Praise for *Bullied: Why You Feel Bad Inside and What to Do About It*

"*Bullied* gently gives readers many of the tools to start pulling themselves out of a situation that can appear hopeless. Mayfield covers why kids become bullies, what to do when parents or teachers are the bullies, and tips for when a student gets so mad he or she feels tempted to hurt someone. Most importantly, she urges the victim to remember that the situation will get better in the future."
—Voice of Youth Advocates

"In less than 100 pages, this book can help people through the challenge of being a bullying victim as well as understand how their own anger can inadvertently cause them to become a bully."
—PsychologyToday.com

"A compelling and insightful expose of the damage bullying can do to a child's self-esteem, and of measures that can be taken to stop it....For anyone who ever found themselves at the mercy of a bully, Mayfield's latest offering is definitely a book to have front and center on your shelves."
—Nashua Telegraph

"This book is a great tool to start the conversation with your kids on what bullying truly looks like and how they can look it straight in the face and fight back. The book is a quick read with inspirational quotes from many well-known figures of our times. I applaud Katherine for rising above her past and being one of those people who seeks to make the path easier for others."
—PowerofMoms.com

"*Bullied: Why You Feel Bad Inside and What to Do About It* is an intriguing and helpful guide for those who have been tormented by bullies, and those who are bullies themselves.... Mayfield's book offers great solace and encouragement for those who may be lacking in confidence and self-esteem caused by being tormented by those who feel the need to take out their frustrations on others."
—BellaOnline.com

Also by Katherine Mayfield

The Box of Daughter: Healing the Authentic Self

*Dysfunctional Families: Exposing the Secrets
Behind Closed Doors*

The Box of Daughter and Other Poems

*Smart Actors, Foolish Choices: A Self-Help Guide
to Coping with the Emotional Stresses of the Business*

*Acting A to Z: A Young Person's Guide to
a Stage or Screen Career*

Bullied

Why You Feel Bad Inside
and
What to Do About It

A Guide to Recovery from Bullying

Katherine Mayfield

Maine Authors Publishing
Rockland, Maine
www.MaineAuthorsPublishing.com

This book is dedicated to:

Bailey O'Neill
Amanda Todd
Ashlynn Conner
Tyler Clementi
Sam Denham
Carl Joseph Walker-Hoover
Amanda Cummings
Brendan Sheehan
Darren Steele
Stephen Shepherd
Kelly Yeomans
Stephen Woodhall
Lynette McLaughlin
Katherine Jane Morrison
Steven Urry
Neil Ross
Jamie Evans
Gail Jones
David Tuck
Laura Grimes
Alistair Hunter
April Himes
Jared High
Ryan Patrick Halligan
Daniel Scruggs
Laura Rhodes
Joshua Melo
Kasey Hone
James Rogers

and the thousands of other teens
who have committed suicide in response to bullying.

Table of Contents

Foreword

Michelle Baker, Director of Education, Blaze My Trail Youth Program

Last summer, I wrote an article called "Bullying Runs Deep." It was the first time I had written directly and openly about being abused by my mother when I was a child, and bullied by my community to keep quiet about it. When Katherine Mayfield wrote to thank me for writing the article, I realized just how important it was to speak up and tell my story, so that others can feel safe enough to tell their stories.

When I was a child in the 1970s, very little was known about how to intervene on behalf of victims of bullying. In fact, it was commonplace to tell kids to tough it out, grow thicker skin, grin and bear it, or to tell them they were making things up.

Some people are still like this today. Why? It's natural to be afraid of bullies. Even grown-ups are afraid of them. After all, what do most bullies say? "You better not tell anyone, or else!" Bullies intimidate their victims by making them feel like they are alone, by making them feel afraid to speak up. So it's very easy to begin to feel like you are indeed alone and no one will understand.

Believe me, I have been there. The principal of my school and a close family friend both told me I was making things up and to stop lying when I went to them for help.

Thankfully, today we have the law and social awareness on our side. From our schools to our homes, bullying is being exposed for what it is: absolutely not ok. It is essential to speak up—or to find someone who will speak up for you when you cannot.

Katherine Mayfield's *Bullied* is a tool to help you identify, confront, and cope with the direct and indirect effects of bullying. Writing from her personal experience and pulling together the experience and insights of others, she has created a user-friendly guide to help you through difficult and scary times.

I dearly wish this book had been available to me, my family, and my school when I was growing up.

If there is one thing I hope you take away from this book, it is to remember in your darkest moments that there is help. Reach out, no matter what it takes. Reach out for help until someone believes you and you get the help you need. You can start right here by reading the stories and looking up the resources in this book.

You deserve a better life. And you are not alone.

~ Michelle Baker, 2013

Introduction

When I was in school, I was bullied not only by other kids, but by my parents as well. Bullying hurts, and sometimes it can make you scared of everything and everyone.

I coped with my feelings by hiding myself way down deep inside. I tried to put on a polite smile and be nice to everyone so no one would hurt me. But they hurt me anyway. I felt like there was no way I could stop it.

Being bullied made me feel like I was helpless, incompetent, and insignificant, because I couldn't figure out a way to stop others from bullying me. I carried those feelings for many years, and eventually they turned into a belief that I *was* that way. Believing that I was helpless and incompetent made me feel miserable, as if I wasn't as good as anyone else. I felt inferior to almost everyone.

Only recently have I begun to understand that those things I believed about myself are not true. It was *the experience of being bullied* that caused me to feel incompetent and insignificant. That's not who I really am inside.

If you're being bullied and you feel that way, too, it's not who you really are, either. Being bullied just makes you feel like you are. And even bullies can have these same kinds of feelings.

> **"It is easy to live for others, everybody does. I call on you to live for yourself."** ~ Ralph Waldo Emerson (essayist, poet, and leader of the Transcendentalist movement of the mid-19th century)

When I became an adult, I still felt inferior, and I was so used to hiding myself and being polite that it became a terrible habit. I was what people used to call a "doormat"—I let others walk all over me—and though I got angry, I never stood up for myself. I thought I was wrong for having feelings. I thought I was defective because I had so many emotions inside, and I didn't know what to do with them. Along with my fear, my anger grew inside of me, unexpressed, until one day I just wanted to end it all.

When I realized I was feeling so bad that I wanted to commit suicide, I decided I needed help. I began therapy, and learned the tools and skills of emotional intelligence, which helped tremendously in coping with my painful feelings. Emotional intelligence means that we are smart about emotions—we learn to understand feelings and how they affect us and others, and find healthy ways to express them that don't hurt anyone, including ourselves.

I discovered in therapy that it felt really good to finally be able to talk about what was going on inside, and have someone help me find a better way to live. I learned easy, harmless ways to express my emotions, and over time, I began to feel lighter and lighter, with feelings of freedom that I'd never had before. And now, I am so much happier than I was when I was struggling with my feelings of hopelessness.

After I had been expressing my feelings for awhile, one day I woke up to see the wonderful, smart, talented person I was deep inside, and I began to heal. You can, too. This book will show you how.

I know there is a wonderful, smart, talented person inside of you, too. So often, we don't get support for the good things we do; we only get criticism for the mistakes we make. Making mistakes is absolutely a normal part of life—they help us learn how to do things better. Our society doesn't encourage us to compliment each other as much as it encourages us to judge and be critical, which is very sad. There are so many people with tremendous potential who never even know what they could do, because their efforts are not supported and encouraged.

> **"Be who God meant you to be and you will set the world on fire."**
> ~ St. Catherine of Siena (patron saint of Italy)

Sometimes parents, too, are not as good as they could be at supporting and encouraging their children, even if they love them. Sometimes they don't know how, and sometimes they're just trying to help their kids be the best they can be, and they think that by criticizing a child, he or she will become a better person. But we all need encouragement and support. Positive reinforcement, such as praise and support, works much better than negative reinforcement and criticism.

This book will show you how to dig under the surface of who you think you are (or who other people have told you that you are), and find the treasure that lies within you, the treasure that lies within each human being: the unique gifts, the intelligence and wisdom, and the potential for happiness that we all have within us. This may sound like a fantasy from where you're at right now, but with time and patience, and by learning to acknowledge and express your feelings, you can begin to achieve whatever you want in your life.

It's very important for you to understand that being bullied doesn't go on forever. Even if you can't feel it right now, there will come a time when you move on in your life and connect with new and different people, and by unearthing and expressing your feelings, you'll be able to create a much happier and more fulfilling life, just as I did.

In this book, you'll learn how to discover and let go of your most difficult emotions. You'll learn how to find the courage to do what you're passionate about, and you'll learn how to start living as the real you, instead of the you that hurts all the time. You'll learn why people turn into bullies, along with some tips for dealing with bullies. And you'll find out that people in other places in the world are different from people in your hometown.

In Part 2, I'll introduce you to a simple four-step plan that will help you feel better fast, and give you some tips for helping yourself to recover from being bullied and raise your self-esteem. You'll also find some stories later in the book from people who have recovered from bullying and gone on to lead happy and productive lives. Throughout the book, there are quotes from famous people—actors, writers, artists, and leading-edge thinkers—which will help you expand your understanding of how other people see life and the world.

This book is meant to be a guide, a companion for you as you begin to explore your feelings. In my head and in my heart, I have been where you probably are now—full of pain and uncertainty, not knowing where to turn, just wishing someone would help. I want to reach out to you with this book, to let you know that someone cares, and offer the help that will get you to a better place.

I wish you peace and comfort, and I encourage you to trust yourself in the process, to listen to your hunches and intuition, to begin to pay more attention to what's going on inside of you instead of what other people are telling you about yourself. There's a part of you that knows how to heal, if you just let it guide you as you read the book.

"Why are you so enchanted by this world, when a mine of gold lies within you?" ~ Rumi (13th century Persian poet and Sufi mystic)

Part 1 – How Bullying Affects Your Feelings and Self-image

How bullying affects you inside

When people put you down, it makes you feel a little smaller, as if you're not as good as they are. You feel like they have power, and you don't. You feel like they must be doing everything right, and everything you do is wrong. But you don't know how to make it all better.

Over time, you may begin to lose your "self-esteem"—your confidence and satisfaction with who you are and how you're living your life—and the emotional pain that builds up can seem overwhelming and unending.

Even if you have these feelings, they are not *who you are*. Feeling small or powerless doesn't mean you *are* that way. If you weren't being bullied, you probably wouldn't have those feelings. If you were being encouraged and supported, you would probably feel strong and confident instead. What makes us feel small and helpless is the experience of being bullied.

You don't need to believe anything a bully says about you. People who bully others often feel out of control and overwhelmed themselves, and they just want to take their anger out on someone else. It doesn't mean that what they're saying is true. If you believe what they say about you, you won't be able to believe in yourself, and it becomes difficult to move forward in your life. You are a good and valuable person, and if you can instead step back and not take the bullying personally (meaning that you don't let it influence your thoughts about yourself), you can help yourself to feel more confident.

"One must still have chaos in oneself to be able to give birth to a dancing star."
~ Friedrich Nietzsche (German philosopher, poet, and composer)

If someone is bullying you based on what you look like—if you're taller or shorter than other people, or if you have braces or glasses, or anything else—they are using one single characteristic about your physical appearance to judge the entirety of who you are. One trait does not define your real self. You are not a nose, or a pair of glasses, or the clothes you wear. Everyone has talents and gifts, and whether you are tall or short or wear braces or glasses, when you focus on your gifts, you can live up to your potential and ultimately become a much happier person.

When I was in school, I wore braces and glasses, and the other kids called me "Metal Mouth" and "Four Eyes." And I was a bookworm, which someone shortened to "Worm" one day. The other kids had a great time with that one! I felt awful every time someone called me "Worm." But at this point in my life, it doesn't bother me that I was called those names, because I know that the kids who called me "Worm" were just trying to feel stronger when they were feeling weak, and wanted to put me down because someone else had put them down. And I know that being a "bookworm" is only part of who I am. In fact, if I hadn't been a bookworm, I probably wouldn't be a writer today.

> **"And you? When will you begin your long journey into yourself?"** ~ Rumi

No one bullies me now, because I've learned how to stand up for myself. I threw the doormat away. Once you become an adult, you will have much more freedom of choice in every aspect of your life. The experience of being bullied really does end, and you can go on to live a much better and happier life.

Bullying is any behavior designed to control and subjugate another person by using fear, humiliation, and repeated verbal assaults. It can include constant criticism, intimidation, belittling, berating, and refusal to ever be pleased. Another name for bullying is "emotional abuse." Bullying can also take physical forms, such as pushing, staring someone down, punching, or physically hurting someone. Bullying is always wrong.

Bullying is similar to brainwashing in that it steadily wears down the victim's self-confidence, sense of self-worth, trust in their own perceptions, and self-esteem. Sometimes the bullying is disguised as "guidance," "teaching," or "advice" (like when someone says, "Don't get your hopes up—your project will never work"), but the results are the same. The recipient of the abuse eventually loses all sense of self, and stops believing in his personal value.

A form of bullying called "verbal abuse" can take the form of blaming, ordering, threatening, and name-calling. Verbal and emotional abusers may invalidate the perceptions of the victim by denying reality when the victim confronts the abuser by saying, "I never did that" or "I never said that," or by telling the victim she doesn't know what she's talking about. People who abuse and bully will not accept responsibility for their actions.

So, how can you cope with being bullied? For centuries, spiritual leaders from all over the globe have told us that by focusing on the *inner world*—what's happening inside of us—we can change the *outer world*, and this is true. In spite of what you may have heard or been taught, other people's opinions don't matter as much as your opinion of yourself. Many people who have grown up in tragic circumstances have used their determination to create a much better life for themselves. They stopped paying so much attention to what was going on around them and what others had told them, and instead began to use a single-minded determination to follow their dreams, no matter what anyone else may have said or done. And they successfully created what they envisioned. You can, too.

> **"Imagine the choices you'd make if you had no fear—of falling, of losing, of being alone, of disapproval."**
> ~ Martha Beck (sociologist, life coach, and bestselling author)

Turning off the outside "chatter" of the world is the way you create a life that works for you. Focusing on what you want to achieve, or what your passion is, is much more important than focusing on what someone else says about you. They can't know who you are inside or how much potential you have to create wonderful things in your life. You may not be able to see it now, but you are a unique individual with a distinctive gift to give to the world. All of us are born with the potential for achievement, because we all look at the world in different ways—your own point of view is the basis for what you have to offer the world, and no one has it but you. Even if you're not feeling supported by others in your life, you can support yourself by starting to believe in yourself, by seeking help if you need it, and by searching for people who are like you and will listen to you.

You may have heard the saying that "you create your own reality." This does not in any way mean that if you're being bullied, you are making it happen. What it means is that the more you focus on your pain and behave in ways that makes your feelings evident to others, the more you are "attracting" painful experiences into your life. If a bully can find someone who already appears to feel helpless and sad, that person is an easy target—and the bully can feel stronger really fast by picking on that person.

The opposite is also true: when you focus on *letting go* of your pain and feeling better, you will create less pain and have more power in your life—and over time, you can eventually become free of the worst of your painful feelings. You can find some helpful books on the subject of "creating your own reality" in the Resource section at the back of this book.

The issue of trust

If you've been bullied a lot, you might have trouble trusting people to be nice to you or to do what they say they're going to do. You might even have trouble trusting yourself. But in my experience—and I've met a lot of people who have been bullied—people who have been victims of bullying usually have a very strong inner sense about who they can trust and who they can't. They're just not used to relying on that intuition. They're still looking outside of themselves for direction.

> "Instinct is the nose of the mind."
> ~ Madame De Girardin
> (French author)

If you pay attention to your instincts, they'll tell you when to stay away from someone, or when someone is a "safe" person to be friends with. Sometimes we get stuck in being as polite as we can to everyone, no matter how they treat us, and then when someone turns out to be unkind or cruel, we kick ourselves because we knew right at the very beginning that we didn't want to be friends.

Sometimes bullies are very, very charming when they first meet you—they may pay you compliments, or act very respectful in the beginning. As you become friends, notice your feelings about the person after you've spent some time together. Do you feel good? Happy with yourself? Did you really enjoy being with that person, and did you feel your friend enjoyed being with you? That's one way to distinguish a "safe" person.

On the other hand, if you feel smaller after you've spent time with them, if you feel like that person is "top dog" and you're "number two," you might want to be more careful as you develop a relationship.

It also takes some time to learn to trust yourself. As I wrote above, it's important to begin learning how to focus on your own thoughts, feelings, and beliefs, and less on others. By doing that, you'll soon

★ ★ ★ ★ ★ ★ ★ ★ ★ ★ ★
"Trust your instinct to the end, though you can render no reason." ~ Ralph Waldo Emerson
★ ★ ★ ★ ★ ★ ★ ★ ★ ★ ★

discover that you can know a little ahead of time when things might get rough—and if you tell yourself, "I can handle it, I will know what to do," you'll begin to develop the capacity to do just that. Some people call this "intuition," and everyone has it. It's just not something we're taught in school. Can you imagine a class called "Intuition 101"? It would certainly help a lot of people figure out where they belong in the world.

When I was young, and being bullied, I always felt like an outsider. I felt like I didn't belong. And this is not an easy feeling to carry with you day after day! But as I found people who were willing to listen to me, and as I learned how to express my feelings, I began to feel as if I was more of an insider—I discovered that I could rely on my own intelligence and intuition instead of what others told me, and I could find ways to do things that worked for me instead of trying to please everyone else. Over time, I began to understand that *most of the people in the world* are pretty supportive and helpful *most of the time*. But when we've had bad experiences and interacted with hurtful people, we expect that to continue. Sometimes people hurt us, and that's a fact we have to learn to live with. But it doesn't mean that there aren't just as many caring, helpful people. We need to be actively looking for the people who will support and help us—and expecting to find them—in order to connect with those people. Sometimes this takes a little time. It's hard to be patient and keep trying, but if you do, you will eventually find supportive people.

Reading inspirational books can be a wonderful way to find help and support—you certainly don't have to worry that the books will hurt you, and you can come back to the most helpful ones again and again. One of the best books I've ever read is *The Drama of the Gifted Child* by Alice Miller. It's a very easy book to read, and will give you a new perspective on who you really are. Ms. Miller believes that every child is gifted—that all of us have potential gifts if we just dig down inside—but that through difficult experiences in the process of growing up, most children's giftedness is covered over by some misguided beliefs they learn from family and friends. You can find out more about Ms. Miller's books in the Resource section.

Next, we'll find out why some kids become bullies.

Why kids become bullies

When people bully someone, they're trying to make themselves feel good. They may feel weak or frightened inside, and think that by bullying someone else, they'll feel stronger. Their put-downs are not a reflection of who you are, but rather an indication that bullies don't feel good about themselves. Sometimes the put-downs are not even based in reality. How could someone else know enough about you to think that they know everything? They don't know who you are inside, and they have no idea what you're capable of.

Bullies sometimes attribute certain qualities to their victims that they feel inside of themselves, but don't want to admit. Psychologists call this "projection," which means that the bully is denying her own feelings of weakness or powerlessness and saying instead that someone else is that way. In order to get rid of those feelings, the bully puts someone else down so that person feels weak or powerless, and then the bully feels stronger.

The bully is "projecting" her flaws or feelings of weakness on the person she bullies, so she doesn't have to deal with her own feelings.

If you're being bullied, try to remember the next time it happens that the bully is only trying to cut you down so he feels bigger—or, to think of it another way, anyone who bullies is simply trying to make you feel as small as he does inside. But you can choose not to take that on by not taking the bully's words and actions personally—remember that their words and actions reflect who *they* are, not who *you* are.

Some bullies just appear to be "mean kids"—they bully everyone they can. But they're often hurting inside. They might have difficult issues to deal with at home, and they might even experience bullying or abuse from others in their family. Most kids who bully have learned how to do it from others, usually people who bully them or other members of their families. Bullies may feel out of control inside, and try to compensate by trying to control others, or they may feel inadequate, and so they put others down to make themselves feel better.

Some bullies are very angry about something in their lives, and don't have a safe place to express their anger. If one of their parents or an older sibling is making them angry or frustrated, it may not feel safe to them to express their anger at that person, so they look for someone else to get angry at—a "scapegoat"—and vent their feelings on that person. This is why bullying often seems so unreasonable and unjustified—because the bully's actions are motivated by some other relationship that has nothing to do with his or her victims.

> **"Do not teach your children never to be angry; teach them how to be angry."**
> ~ Lyman Abbott (American Congregationalist theologian and author)

If a bully lives in a very strict household, he or she probably believes that the best way to live is to try to control others. In that sense, they are probably mimicking their parents. Bullies sometimes exert control over others because they are feeling controlled by someone else, and the urge to control something—anything—in their lives is so strong that they begin bullying others.

All of this information is not meant to make you feel sorry for bullies. I've only included it here so you can understand that bullies often feel inadequate and powerless inside—which means that they are not as strong or powerful or perfect as you might think they are.

When parents are bullies

"It behooves a father to be blameless if he expects his child to be."
~ Homer (considered to be the greatest of the Greek epic poets)

Sometimes parents or other caregivers are bullies. We come into the world as babies, totally helpless, totally dependent on the people who are there to care for us. We don't have any way of knowing whether what they're doing and how they treat us is right or wrong, because we have nothing to compare it to.

Parents may criticize their children, telling them (or showing them with facial expressions or body language) that they're not doing things right. They may put their kids down. For instance, if a girl comes up with a wonderful idea for a science project at school, they may obviously or subtly let her know that they don't think she can handle the project, or that girls aren't supposed to be interested in science, or that the idea won't work. When this kind of criticizing or belittling goes on for a long time—for weeks, or years, or even a young person's entire life—the experience of being put down can become so familiar that it seems as if that's just the way life is. But it's not. There are many, many supportive people in the world, just as there are many dysfunctional families. When we become adults, we're much more able to choose the people we want to be with and be in relationship with, and to limit the time we spend with dysfunctional or hurtful people.

Most parents don't consciously try to put their children down—some of them just learned from their own parents that it's the way to bring children up. Other parents are trying to help their kids succeed, and are just going about it in an ineffective way. There are also some parents who sense that their kids are very intelligent and/or creative, and it feels threatening to them, so they criticize and demean the kids in order to feel a little stronger inside—just like bullies at school bully other kids so they can feel more powerful.

If your parents have criticized you a lot, it will feel so familiar to you that it seems "normal" to be put down. This makes it difficult to respond to a bully at school in an assertive way, because you're so used to being unable to protect yourself from your parents' criticism. It's absolutely normal for kids to think they have to put up with everything their parents dish out, because they're afraid that if they don't, their parents will abandon them. So if they are bullied at school, it feels as if they can't do anything about it. But they can. You can learn how to protect yourself. If this is happening to you, check out the Tips for Coping with Bullies section later in the book.

Now you know why some kids become bullies—because they feel inadequate, or because their parents are bullying them, and so bullying feels normal to them.

> **"If children grew up according to early indications, we should have nothing but geniuses."**
> ~ Johann Wolfgang von Goethe (German poet)

If you think your parents are bullying you, find someone to talk to as soon as you can—a school counselor or nurse, or a teacher that you trust. You can start by telling them that you're not getting the support you need at home, and you'd like to know if you could talk with them from time to time, or if they could help you find someone who will listen. Let them know that your home situation is causing you to feel bad about yourself and your life. You can tell them you don't want your parents to know you asked for help. If the first person you go to won't help, try someone else. If that person won't help, try someone else. So often we get discouraged because we don't receive the help we need when we first ask for it—but sometimes it takes time to find people who will listen.

You'll find a list of phrases you can use to ask for help in Part 2 of this book.

If this is your situation, you're not alone. Lots of kids have parents who don't support them in the ways they need to be supported. Most people don't talk about the difficulties they have in their families, so we don't know that similar experiences happen to others, too. We think others are doing just fine, when in reality, many of them are hiding the same kinds of feelings that we are. It's almost a tradition in some families to keep all of the pain and distress and hurt "behind closed doors" so that the family looks more functional when they're in public.

In my family, we kept all our problems at home, and put on social masks when we went out. When we were in public, we appeared to be a "perfect" family—very polite, very functional, very helpful to other people. Everyone outside the family thought we were really together, and many people in the community looked up to my parents. But at home, when there was no one else around, there was a lot of conflict and abuse, and daily life there was often chaotic and confusing.

Until I became an adult, I thought all families were just like mine. Until I moved to a different city, I thought all people were like the people I grew up with. But over time, I discovered that people are very different in different cities, towns, and countries, and every family has a different set of dynamics. There are families who are loving toward each other, who help each other, and who respect each others' rights.

It took me a long time to ask for help—and during that time, I was positive that my situation could never get any better. But when I finally found a counselor who would listen to me talk about

> **"Most men lead lives of quiet desperation and go to the grave with the song still in them."**
> ~ Henry David Thoreau (American author, poet, philosopher, abolitionist, naturalist, tax resister, historian, and leading transcendentalist)

my feelings and what was going on, the difference in how I began to view myself and my life was amazing! She helped me to see the whole situation from a more realistic point of view, and helped me understand that the critical comments my parents had always made went way above and beyond the normal process of teaching children about life and keeping them safe from harm. My parents' belittling was constant, and very hurtful to my self-esteem. The counselor helped me learn that I was smart and capable—that it was just *the experience of being bullied* that made me feel defective and incompetent. And she gave me some tools that helped me to change my life for the better.

My parents bullied me, and I felt very angry, sad, and frustrated about it. If you are having these feelings about things that are happening at home, and if you think that bullying may be the reason, there are many things you can do to help yourself feel better and recover from the experience. Along with finding someone who will help you understand what's going on and who will listen to you talk about how you're feeling, there are things you can do yourself on your own. For starters, you can look up "parental bullying" on the net.

First we'll talk a bit about feelings, and then you'll learn more practical steps you can take to help yourself feel better.

Feelings are absolutely normal

Experiencing emotions is an entirely normal aspect of being a human being. Most people in our society don't express feelings, or they don't express them very much or very often. This makes those of us who have *lots* of feelings think that we're strange, or, as my mother used to say, "too sensitive." There is absolutely nothing wrong with having feelings. They are nature's way of helping us protect ourselves and understand ourselves in relation to the world. Feelings let us know when someone has invaded our personal space, or when someone is behaving in a way that's not appropriate or respectful.

The feeling of fear usually occurs when someone has threatened us with words or with facial expressions and body language. Anger often occurs when we are repeatedly mistreated or disrespected, and we don't have a way to stop that behavior. Sadness arises when we need something from others, but no matter how hard we try, we can't seem to get the support or encouragement that we needed.

All of these feelings are completely normal. Some babies are born with a large capacity for emotions; some are born with less. Some kids develop a "thick skin" as they grow up, so nothing really bothers them, and others are more vulnerable to what others say and do. There's no reason to try to be different, because you are exactly right just the way you are—but if you feel like you're sensitive to what others say and do, you need to learn how to manage your sensitivity and the resulting emotions so they don't become overwhelming. The next section will help you learn how to do just that.

Part 2 – How to Feel Better:
The Four-Step Plan for Recovering

This is a plan for helping you understand your feelings and express them in healthy ways. When we don't express our feelings, their energy can seem to grow bigger and bigger and bigger until we're just overwhelmed with feelings, thinking that nothing will ever change and that there's no way out of the situation.

The best way to feel better is to make friends with your feelings instead of trying to push them away. When you push them away, they don't really go away—they keep coming back and bothering you, because they need to be expressed. People don't learn about feelings in school the way they learn about reading, math, and science, but feelings are a very important part of being human, just like eating and getting exercise.

> **"Allowing children to show their guilt, show their grief, show their anger, takes the sting out of the situation."**
> ~ Martha Beck

Expressing feelings is like letting the steam out of a pressure cooker. If the steam were to build up and build up without being released little by little, eventually the pressure cooker would explode—which is what people often do when they let their emotions build up and don't release them over time.

Four simple steps to help you feel better

Here's a quick outline of the four steps you can use to help yourself feel better. I'll explain them more in depth later in this section, and you'll get a chance to try them out for yourself.

The first step in feeling better is looking inside to find out exactly what it is you're feeling. Is it shame? Sadness? Anger? Despair? See if you can put a name to what you're feeling.

The second step is to express whatever it is that you're feeling. For example, if you're sad, you might cry. If you're mad, you could go to the gym and work out on the punching bag, or grit your teeth and shake your fists. Following this section are some suggestions for expressing each type of emotion.

The third step is to tell yourself that you can let go of that emotion. When we're afraid to express emotions, or don't know how, we sometimes hold on to them instead of letting them go, so they continue to make us feel bad even after we've noticed them. Imagine that you have your fist clenched around some tiny, sharp rocks. They'll continue to hurt your hand as long as you're holding them. But if you open your hand and let them go, your hand will feel better almost instantly, and it can begin to heal. You can do the same thing by allowing your feelings to float out of your energy field.

After you've expressed your feelings, the fourth step is to move on and find something fun to do, like getting together with friends or going to a movie—do something that makes you feel better, like going for a walk in your favorite place or spending time with a pet.

"The soul would have no rainbow had the eyes no tears."
~ John Vance Cheney (American poet and essayist)

Being bullied can cause many different kinds of feelings. Along with other emotions, many people feel ashamed when they're bullied, as if they've done something wrong, even though they haven't. Shame is a natural feeling in that it helps us know when we've done something wrong, or hurt another person. Another word for it is "conscience." But when other people criticize us and put us down, we can develop "unhealthy shame," which is shame that is not based on who we really are or how we behave—it's based on believing that we're wrong or defective, because someone else has said so.

This kind of unhealthy shame is an error in our thinking. We stop looking inside and seeing the good parts of ourselves, and begin to focus on what other people say about us. Knowing that their taunts and ridicule come from an unhealthy place within *them* allows us to see that the comments they make are probably untrue, because the words are based on their own distorted perceptions, and not on who we are inside.

Sadness, anger, and despair are more authentic emotions—they are natural human responses to being threatened or humiliated. Fear is also an authentic emotion, and it can be amplified by previous experiences you've had where you felt threatened (such as memories of being yelled at as a child). These memories can be "triggered" by your current experiences—which means that the feelings associated with the memory can pop up unexpectedly in your mind and body in response to a current situation. Which emotions feel the strongest inside of you?

When you've figured out which of your emotions are the biggest at this point, the next step is to express some of that emotion, and get it out of your system. People used to call this "getting something off your chest"—which makes sense, because you are releasing a difficult emotion from your heart.

If there's someone in your life with whom you feel comfortable expressing your feelings, ask that person if they can spend some time listening to you—not to offer suggestions or try to help you solve a problem, but just to listen, so you can "vent" your emotions as you need to. This person should be a good listener who you know will give you space to talk when you need it, someone who makes you feel safe.

If there's no one in your life like this, you can express your feelings in private, someplace where you feel safe and know you won't be disturbed. In this case, imagine that a part of you will act as a "witness" to your feelings—as if you're being a friend to yourself while you express your feelings. You could think of the "witness" as your soul, or a higher power, or the memory of a grandmother or other person who helped you feel safe and loved. The idea is that part of you can stand outside of what you're thinking and feeling, as if you're watching what goes on inside of you from another perspective. This aspect of you is different from the part of you that thinks and feels and remembers. Some people might call it your spirit, and sometimes it can be represented by an imaginary friend.

When I was a child, I imagined that there was a really short guy dressed in a dilapidated suit and hat following me around with a pencil and paper, recording everything that happened. I didn't try to imagine him or make him up, he was just there. We never had any contact—he never looked at me, and we never talked—but I often "felt" him as if I saw someone out of the corner of my eye. I always knew he wasn't real, but it was comforting to imagine that someone knew about everything that I experienced. When I grew up, I realized that he was a manifestation of the "witness" aspect of my psyche.

You can get a feeling for your "witness" by pretending for a moment that you are a friend of yours, instead of yourself. Say your name, and imagine that the person who belongs to that name is standing in front of you, instead of inside you. Imagine that all of your thoughts, feelings, and memories belong to that person for a moment, instead of to you. See what it feels like to be "outside yourself." If it's frightening to you, remember that you can "take yourself back" at any time.

When you focus on expressing your feelings, try to have at least a tiny part of you standing apart, like a witness to what you're experiencing.

"What soap is for the body, tears are for the soul."

~ Jewish Proverb

Here are some ways to express your emotions:

Sadness, Despair, or Depression—Feeling Like There's No Hope

The important thing to remember about sadness and despair is that they don't go on forever. When you're in the midst of feeling them, it seems like the feelings will never end. But they do. Life changes over time—you'll graduate from school, and go on to college or out into the world to work, and at that point you'll be with new people, make new friends, and have new experiences.

One way to give yourself a taste of what it will be like to have your life change is to do one new thing every day: window-shop in a new store, try a new hobby, ask a new person to sit with you at lunch or to walk home from school with you. These are the kinds of experiences that you can pursue in order to "feed yourself," or as some people say, "feed your soul." New experiences can give you happiness, offer you a new way of seeing things, and provide opportunities to meet new people and get some of the things you may not be getting in other ways in your life.

It's extremely important to learn how to nourish yourself in this way—whether you enjoy getting out and meeting people, or prefer reading books or doing puzzles. Whatever makes you feel good is a tool you can use often to nourish yourself.

The more you nourish yourself, and do things that you enjoy and are good at, the more your self-esteem and confidence will grow.

Sadness and despair do have an ending, and the more you can express these feelings, the less they will bother you. Try these suggestions:

1. Go to a movie with a couple of packages of Kleenex, sit in the back if you want, and let yourself cry at the sad parts. When you can finally let yourself cry and release your hurt feelings, it may seem like you want to cry a lot—but that's because you've been saving up the tears for years. It's perfectly normal to cry when we're hurt, even as adults.

2. Hold a pet or a stuffed animal, and imagine that it is pouring all the love you ever wanted into your heart.

3. Get some acrylic paints and art paper, and paint your feelings onto the paper. Even if all you want to paint is smears of dark colors, painting or drawing is a very effective way to release emotions, and it also works well for anger and fear. You don't have to be a good artist, and it doesn't matter what the picture looks like. The important thing is that it helps you let go of difficult feelings.

4. Whether or not you think you can write, it's really helpful to write about your feelings in a journal. Write as if there is someone listening who is very caring, and understands exactly how you feel. You might even try some simple poems. If you're afraid of someone finding your writing, write on the computer, and don't save your words, or write it in a secret code that no one but you will understand. Just the process of putting feelings into words gets them out of your head, and you'll be able to see everything more clearly.

5. Regular exercise can help you feel better quickly. Moving your body helps you let go of "stuck" energy, and releases feel-good brain chemicals. You don't have to join a gym or class—you can just turn on the radio and dance, however it feels right to

you. If feelings come up while you exercise, accept them and express them if you can: make fists and swing your arms while you're walking, or let your body express your feelings when you dance.

6. Volunteering helps some people work through their feelings. You might not cry while you volunteer, but you're still healing your heart by being with other people. If you like animals, you could spend one day a week at an animal shelter. If you love books, perhaps you could volunteer at the library on a Saturday afternoon. Most people who work at libraries are very kind and caring. Volunteering is a way to "feed yourself"—to nourish your need to belong, to be appreciated and respected.

7. Another way to "feed yourself" is by meditating. Meditating doesn't have to be a weird practice where you sit on the floor in a certain posture or chant or have some kind of mystical experience. Meditating can be your time to give yourself what you need. When the world is overwhelming, you can sit down and stop "doing" for awhile, and even pull in energy from the universe. There is so much that needs to be done in life that sometimes we get used to putting all our energy out into tasks and relationships that we forget to take energy in. Life becomes like breathing out, but forgetting to breathe in. In the Appendix, you'll find a short meditation to nurture yourself that you can use anywhere when you have a moment to be quiet.

> **"We have all a better guide in ourselves, if we would attend to it, than any other person can be."**
> ~ Jane Austen (English novelist)

Some people replenish themselves best by going within, by focusing on their inner world. Other people find pleasure in getting together with friends to laugh and have fun, and to enjoy each other's company, but most people also need alone time to think and dream. The world demands a lot of our attention and energy, especially during the school years. By meditating or spending some time every day focusing on our inner selves, by giving ourselves attention, we can heal a lot of the pain we carry around from day to day.

If none of these ideas work for you, and you feel stuck in sadness and despair, it's vital that you find someone to talk with—a friend, a school counselor, a teacher, a therapist. We are not meant to live filled to the brim with pain all the time, and there are many options for feeling better. You can also Google "teen depression" and "teen support" for forums and hotlines. You'll find a list of hotlines later on in the book.

The first time I started letting go of my sadness, I thought I would cry forever—it felt as if the tears would never stop. But the body has a way of letting you know when it's done for the time being. You might

> **"Memory is always faulty. Emotions are always true."**
> ~ Author Unknown

yawn after you cry, or the world around you might look a little brighter. Over time, as you let go of more and more of your sadness, you'll begin to have days where you actually feel pretty good. And at some point, most of the worst of your sadness and despair will have been released, and you'll feel much more hopeful about your life.

One more suggestion: Food allergies have been known to cause mood swings, depression, and a sense of hopelessness. For some people, removing a certain food, like eggs, wheat, corn, dairy, or nuts can make a huge difference in the way they feel emotionally. There's more information on this subject near the end of this section.

Anger

Anger is also a normal human feeling. We get angry because someone has hurt us or invaded our space, or somehow treated us in a way that is insulting or damaging. It's very important to express feelings of anger, because if we don't, they build up over time into resentment and bitterness—and the longer this goes on, the more difficult it is to make positive changes in your life. Road rage—when someone explodes in violent anger for a very slight offense by another driver—is an example of what happens when an adult lets anger build up for a long time without expressing it.

If you're mad, it probably means that someone has hurt or insulted you in some way. Some people use their anger to try to get back at other people, but this usually causes more hurt and insults on the part of both people, so it isn't a very effective way to deal with anger. Retaliation only makes things worse for everyone involved.

Here are some safe and healthy ways you can express your anger, so you don't hurt yourself or anyone else:

1. The best way to release anger is through some form of physical action: chopping wood, throwing rocks in a river, shaking your fists, punching sofa pillows. Some people go to the gym and work out in order to let go of their anger; some people become runners or participate in a sport that allows their bodies to let go of the massive energy that anger creates. Kickball—or even just kicking a ball around on the playground—is a great way to release anger. Even if you start off feeling like it's a stupid thing to do, your body will show you pretty quickly what it wants to do to let go of the anger.

2. If you're in a place where you can't take time to express the anger physically, here's a quick tip: go to the restroom and do some silent screaming—let your body act as if you're really screaming in anger, but do it silently. Clench your fists, open your mouth wide, and pretend you're screaming. The important thing is to feel the anger leaving your body as you silently scream, and to give yourself support for acknowledging and expressing your feelings in a healthy way.

• • • • • •

"When you do things from your soul, you feel a river moving in you, a joy."
~ Rumi

• • • • • •

3. Art is good for expressing anger as well as sadness. Let your feelings come out through your hands onto the page—use lots of red or black, or whatever colors best express your anger. You don't have to paint a "picture"; the objective is simply to get your feelings out onto the paper so they're not running around in circles in your head. Try finger painting. Use your whole hand to paint. Add words to your picture along with images. It doesn't matter what the picture ends up looking like. All that matters in this exercise is getting your feelings out.

4. If you love sports or working out, this is a great way to express anger, though it's in a slightly different form. Before a practice or game, think about things that make you feel angry, and let them fuel your physical energy so that you're releasing

anger as you shoot baskets or hit the hockey puck. Don't carry your anger into the game so that you're whacking the puck or flinging the ball around or getting mad at other players, because you won't play as well as you do when you're focused on the game. Just let the anger act as fuel for your game, and you may play even better than you usually do.

5. Regular exercise is a great outlet for anger. Moving your body helps you let go of "stuck" energy, and releases feel-good brain chemicals. Even going for a walk can help you feel better quickly. If feelings come up while you exercise, accept them and express them if you can. While you're walking, imagine yourself saying the words you'd really like to say to someone who has made you angry, and let the energy fuel your body as you walk.

If none of these ideas work for you, and you feel stuck in your anger or want to hurt someone else, or yourself, it's very important that you find someone to talk with—a friend, a school counselor, a teacher, or a therapist. There are many options for managing anger.

Here are a couple of websites to check out:
http://teenadvice.about.com/od/violencebullying/a/angermana gement.htm and
http://www.youngwomenshealth.org/anger.html.

Food allergies have been known to cause mood swings, aggression, and even a sense of feeling angry, as well as creating a bodily response of anxiety. For some people, removing a certain food, like eggs, wheat, corn, dairy, or nuts can make a huge difference in the way they feel emotionally. There's more information on this subject near the end of this section.

Fear

I'm a nervous type myself, so I have a lot of experience with fear. If you have a history of trauma or abuse, your top priority is to help yourself feel safe, most especially when expressing your feelings.

You might think it's silly to "give in to your fears"—and someone may have even told you that. Nobody

"Fear is static that prevents me from hearing myself."
~ Samuel Butler (Victorian author in England)

likes to be called a "scaredy-cat." But just like anger, our fear is there for a reason. Either we've been hurt in some way, or we feel threatened by someone or some experience.

Remember that some people are more sensitive than others. If you're a sensitive person, it can be difficult just to experience the world every day with all its busyness and activity. In the Resource section, there are some books on how to manage sensitivity, which may help you cope better with life. Being gentle with yourself is the best way to help yourself overcome your fear. Threatening yourself, pushing your fear away, or thinking you have to just "deal with it" can actually make the fear worse. Fear doesn't go away if you try to ignore it.

Try these tips for letting go of your fear:

1. Deep breathing: when we become fearful, our breathing gets more and more shallow, and when our cells are deprived of oxygen, they send a message to the brain of fear for survival. Try to let the breath just "drop in" to your belly, and "fall out" when you breathe out.

2. Consider some form of yoga, or a martial art like Tai Chi. Qi Gong is another very effective method for getting more grounded and relaxed, and helps to quiet thoughts and anxious physical reactions. If there aren't any classes near you, you can Google "Qi Gong Demonstration" and watch some videos. I've found Qi Gong to be invaluable in helping me face life more peacefully.

"Fear makes the wolf bigger than he is." ~ German proverb

3. If you can find a private place, it often helps a lot to shake your hands, as if you're shaking water off to dry them. Sometimes it helps to shake your whole body. Your body will let you know what it wants to do to let go of the fear if you listen to it. Think about a toddler who has lost his mother in the mall—when he finally finds her, he shakes and cries, and releases his fear. Five minutes later, he may be laughing again—he's free to experience the next moment because he has let go of his overwhelming emotions.

4. Listen to music that makes you feel strong and powerful. Let your body respond to the music in whatever way it wants

to—dancing, raising your arms like a god, or jumping up and down.

5. Exercise can help you feel less anxious and fearful. Moving your body helps you let go of "stuck" energy, and releases feel-good brain chemicals. Pick some form of exercise that helps you feel safe, like walking or strength training, or you can just turn on the radio and dance, however it feels right to you. If feelings come up while you exercise, accept them and express them if you can.

If none of these ideas work for you, and you feel stuck in anxiety and fear, it's essential that you find someone to talk with—a friend, a school counselor, a teacher, a therapist. A life lived in fear is a life in which potential is never reached, and there are many options for feeling better. Here's a great video that can help you calm down fast: go to http://ow.ly/i6nJ3 and click on the top video.

> **"The sorrow which has no vent in tears may make other organs weep."**
> ~ Henry Maudsley (pioneering British psychiatrist)

Alice Miller is a wonderful author who wrote a number of books on releasing feelings. One of them was titled *The Body Never Lies*, in which she writes that even though we may believe that we can get past our emotions without experiencing and letting go of them, our bodies know that we're bottling them up. This is sometimes why people get cancer or heart disease later in life—because they've bottled up all of their emotions, and the stress of trying to cover up feelings takes a huge toll on the body's health. *The Body Never Lies* is a great book which will help you understand how your body can teach you to let go of overwhelming feelings.

Alice Miller has written many great books on how we can stop listening to what others say, and tune into our own wisdom. Reading her books will start you on a wonderful journey of self-discovery—you'll find that there is a wonderful self within you that isn't based at all on what others say about you.

How food allergies and color can affect our feelings

Research suggests that food allergies and intolerances can cause depression, mood swings, and other emotional symptoms—even aggression, anger, and fear. Emotions are related to the biochemistry of the body (the way the various nutrients and chemicals react in our brains). I discovered that by giving up certain foods to which I was sensitive, my mood lifted, and I felt much more optimistic about myself and my life.

Years after that, I found that even citric acid, for whatever reason, made me extremely anxious, and I discovered that many, many products contain this allergen. Once I stopped using products that contained citric acid, the difference in my confidence was awesome. Some people experience a feeling of anger and rage when they ingest something with citric acid in it. You do have to read labels when you're trying to pinpoint food allergies, but the results are totally worth it.

Searching for allergy sites on the web can tell you if you have symptoms of food allergies. Here are two websites to get you started:
http://www.allergy-details.com/allergy-symptoms/allergies-and-mood/ and
http://www.soulwork.net/sw_articles_eng/food-allergy.htm

If you think you might have food allergies, you can find out by eliminating foods like dairy, wheat, corn, nuts, and soy for two weeks, and then begin introducing one food at a time so you can see whether your symptoms recur. It's best to choose one food at a time to try, so you can figure out exactly which one is causing your problem. This is called an elimination diet—and there's information about it on the net.

Other physical challenges that can cause depression are low blood pressure, mono, Epstein-Barr, Lyme disease, and chronic fatigue. Anger and frustration can be caused by high blood pressure. The next time you visit your doctor, ask if there could be any health issues that might be making you depressed or frequently angry.

Colors can also affect your mood. If your bedroom is decorated in mostly dark colors, you may be too "yin"—a

Chinese word meaning that the energy around you encourages you to be withdrawn and have low energy. Try adding some yellow, red, and orange to your room, and do some research on the principles of "yin and yang."

If your home or bedroom is decorated in very bright colors, like red, orange, or yellow, the environment could be too "yang" for you. "Yang" is a Chinese word meaning that the energy around you is overstimulating. Try wearing blue or green-colored clothes, and spending some time in your room with the lights turned down. You could also do some research on the principles of "yin and yang."

> **"Emotions have taught mankind to reason."**
> ~ Marquis De Vauvenargues (French writer and moralist)

Summary of the four steps

So here is a summary of the four steps you can take to cope with your feelings:

1. Acknowledge what you're feeling—is it shame? Sadness? Despair? Anger?

2. Find a private place, and let yourself express that feeling: cry, punch sofa pillows, shake your fists, throw rocks into a pond—whatever helps. Let your body do what it wants to do

3. Tell yourself you can let go of that feeling. You don't have to keep holding it inside. Call up the witness part of you to comfort yourself as you express your emotions, and remind yourself that what you're feeling is not *who you are*, it's only a feeling that will pass.

4. After you've let go of some feelings, call a supportive friend to talk about something else, go to a movie, or join a group that's going to a fun place—just so you help yourself remember that life can be good. Anything you enjoy doing is fine. After you've expressed some of your feelings, try to forget about them and what caused them while you go pursue a good time. If you're not good at making friends, do something else that you really enjoy,

like playing with your cat or taking a long walk or going to the library.

When someone hurts us, it's human nature to hold on to the hurt, because we think that somehow, if we can figure it out, it won't be as painful. But you hurt yourself all over again when you hold on to a bad feeling—thinking about past experiences can drag you down and make you miserable over time. It feels much better to let them go, just let their energy drift out of your body and mind—and once you do, you can see everything a little more clearly.

> **"The deeper that sorrow carves into your being, the more joy you can contain."**
> ~ Kahlil Gibran (Lebanese-American artist, poet, and writer)

Letting go is a process, not something you do just once and you're done. If the pain keeps coming up, that just means you haven't quite let go of all of it yet. Each time you feel it, focus on letting it go, noticing what it's about as you let it dissolve. If you do this enough times, the pain will be gone, and the experience attached to it will become integrated (meaning that it will be part of your memories, but not in the same painful way). It's like learning something in school: sometimes you have to use a new word a few times in order to make it part of your vocabulary, or work a math problem over and over to understand the principle behind it. Once you let the pain go, you're freeing up a lot of your mind's energy to choose things that make you happier.

To the best of your ability, once you've expressed the feelings surrounding the hurt, let go of the experience, and fill your thoughts instead with what you'd rather have in your life, or with new possibilities that you can glimpse on the horizon. How would you like your life to be? The more you think about what you want, the more likely it is that opportunities to make that happen will come to you. This is part of a practice called "Creative Visualization," in which you learn how to imagine life the way you would like it to be, and send energy to your vision. What you focus on expands—so keep your focus on moving forward into feeling better as much as you can.

See if you can find a book called *Creative Visualization* by Shakti Gawain. This book will help you turn your life around by teaching you how to visualize what you want to create in your life.

How to ask for help

Human beings are not supposed to feel bad all the time. Even if you've been taught that you "shouldn't have feelings," it's absolutely normal to feel sad, angry, or lost at times and to ask for help in dealing with your emotions. If you feel overwhelmed by your feelings, it's very important to reach out for help. Though there are a lot of useful online resources, reaching out to a real person will give you more of a connection and more hope than visiting Internet sites.

When you approach someone for help, make sure you know that the person is a "safe" person—that they will at least listen to you, and won't cause you any more pain by telling you that "You shouldn't feel that way" or "Maybe you should do your homework instead." If there's a teacher or school counselor with whom you feel you have a good connection, that person is a good place to start. If someone responds to your request with one of the statements above, it probably means they don't like to examine and deal with their own emotions, so listening to yours would be hard for them. Keep looking for someone who will genuinely listen.

If you have a friend or sibling you know you can trust, start with that person. Even though most people don't talk about their feelings regularly, there are people who are fairly open to discussing feelings, especially if you let them know you're having difficulties with your emotions. Everyone has emotions—many people have *strong* emotions—but unfortunately, it's not something most people are used to talking about.

If the first person you reach out to won't listen or help, try another. And keep trying until you find someone who will listen. There are many, many people who are willing to help others in any way they can.

If you go to church, and you feel comfortable with the minister, ask if you could meet briefly with him or her. If you know of a church that has a youth program in your area, there may be a youth minister who is more open to talking about teen issues than a regular minister.

If you don't have anyone you feel you can trust, go to a hospital and tell them you're having some feelings that are overwhelming, and you'd like help finding some resources. Going to a hospital doesn't mean you're crazy—it's just a good place to find out about more resources. Ask if there's a counseling center near you.

> "To know what you prefer, instead of humbly saying 'Amen' to what the world tells you you ought to prefer, is to keep your soul alive." ~Robert Louis Stevenson (Scottish novelist, poet, essayist)

Sometimes we're more comfortable talking about our emotions with strangers than we are with family, friends, or other people we know. This is why a lot of people see therapists—they choose to talk about their problems in private so they can go about their daily lives with more confidence and clarity. There are about 93,000 therapists in the U.S., so you know a lot of people must be going to see them! Sadly, in our country, acknowledging and expressing emotions is still thought of as something we should do "behind closed doors," usually with a therapist. That's one of the reasons you don't see many people expressing feelings in public.

You can find out more about what therapy is like by watching *In Treatment*, which was an HBO series—just search the web for "In Treatment HBO series" to find out more about it. This series is available from Netflix.

Talking with a therapist is often extremely helpful for young people who are going through a bad time. A therapist can help you put a situation into a better perspective, and can give you tools for coping with problems in your life. Seeing a therapist is like having someone who's always on your side, always wanting to help you feel better—they can help you in many, many ways. You may not find a perfect fit with the first person you see. Remember that you have good instincts, and you'll know when you connect with the right person.

Here are some phrases you could use to approach someone for help:

1. I'm having some feelings that are overwhelming, and I'd like to find someone who will listen to me for a bit, or find some resources. Can you help me for a moment?

2. Do you know of any resources for coping with sadness and anger, or anxiety?

3. A friend of mine suggested that I talk with you about my feelings. Do you have a few minutes to talk, or is there some time I can come back?

4. I'm a little confused about something, and I'd like to get feedback from you. Could I talk with you sometime?

If you're having trouble coping with a bully, be sure to mention that in your conversation. Some schools also have drop-boxes where you can report an incident. If you don't know what your school's policy is on anti-bullying, go to the school office and ask.

Remember that you may have to ask several people before you find someone who will help. It isn't because they don't want to help you—it's probably because everyone is so busy, and most people are just trying to get through the day (just like you). If you reach out to several people and can't find anyone, be a little more firm: "I need to talk." Be persistent. It is an incredible relief to have someone listen when you need to talk—and an incredible relief to have someone validate your feelings in person.

If you still can't seem to find anyone, try calling a teen hotline, such as teenlineonline.org. There are more hotlines listed on the next few pages.

"We are healed from suffering only by experiencing it to the full." Marcel Proust (French novelist and author)

If you're thinking about suicide

Sometimes the idea of suicide can seem like it's the only answer to all of your problems. You may feel helpless to control anything in your life, and you may have a feeling of hopelessness, thinking that things will never change and you will never feel better. You might think you're crazy, or that you're going crazy. You're not. Most people have these kinds of feelings at some point in their lives, so you aren't alone. You may not think that others have these feelings, because people generally don't express them—instead, they project an image of confidence, and don't talk about what's under the surface. But everyone feels powerless and helpless now and then.

> **"Sometimes even to live is an act of courage."**
> ~ Lucius Annaeus Seneca (Roman philosopher and statesman)

Some people appear very strong and confident almost all the time, and it's easy to assume that that's "who they are." For decades, if not centuries, our culture has encouraged its citizens to ignore or deny feelings—or if we do experience them, to keep them hidden—and to project a tough, self-assured image. So when people are "out in public," they're not usually allowing the more emotional, vulnerable parts of themselves to show. But this certainly doesn't mean that they don't have emotions or feel vulnerable. It's just that our culture trains us to show only the strong side. What people show on the outside isn't necessarily what they're experiencing on the inside. You may even have experienced "putting up a good front" yourself when you're having a difficult time. Always remember that others have feelings too, sometimes difficult ones, even if you don't see them express those feelings.

Feelings of helplessness can make us think that we're not worth anything. But every human being has something unique to offer. If you feel like you're not worth anything, then you probably haven't yet found what it is you're really good at. Or if you have, you might feel like it's not enough. You might want to read some of the interviews at the end of the book—you'll find that other people have felt just about as bad as you probably do, and they were able over time to lift themselves out of their depression and sadness.

Every human being has a right to the best life they can create, and we all have something to offer. Just the fact that you are living and breathing in the world means that you have a right to a good life, and that you're okay just as you are for right now. Life can and will get better.

When your feelings are overwhelming and you just want to get away from them, this is the perfect time to ask for help. You can use the sentences above, or come up with your own ideas about how to ask. Even if you feel hopeless a lot of the time, by using the ideas and tips in this book, you'll feel better as time goes by.

Many people have gone through hopeless times in their lives, but found that things got better as time went by. It's hard to believe that when you're in a bad space, but it is true. Life is a series of ups and downs, and though we don't like it, sometimes we have to hit bottom before things start looking up, and then we can rebuild our lives in a much better way.

Victor Frankl wrote about his efforts to stay positive in the midst of the horrors of the Holocaust in his book *Man's Search for Meaning*. There are many examples of people who have lived through horrible times, and eventually found their way to better lives. It is absolutely possible for you to do the same.

Calling a hotline is a good first step toward feeling better. When you call a hotline, you can be anonymous—no one knows who you are, you don't have to meet someone face to face, and you'll be reaching out to people who absolutely want to help you feel better. The fact that there are so many of these hotlines shows that there are many, many people who want you to reach out, who want to help you, as well as many, many people who seek out their help.

> **"The greatest danger, that of losing one's own self, may pass off quietly as if it were nothing."**
> ~ Soren Kierkegaard (Danish philosopher and theologian, generally recognized as the first existentialist philosopher)

Here are some resources for when you feel like you just want out:

Covenant House Nineline: 1-800-999-9999
Hopeline: 1-800-442-HOPE
National Adolescent Suicide Hotline: 1-800-621-4000
Teen Suicide Prevention Hotline: 1-800-949-0057
24-hour national crisis hotline: 1-800-448-3000
1-800-SUICIDE (1-800-784-2433)
1-800-273-TALK (1-800-273-8255)

Youthline: 1-877-YOUTHLINE (1-877-968-8454) teen-to-teen peer counseling hotline

Hotlines for Specific Groups:
LGBT Youth Suicide Hotline: 1-866-4-U-TREVOR
Suicide Hotline in Spanish: 1-800-273-TALK (Press 2)
Boys Town: 1-800-448-3000

Outside of the U.S.:
24-Hour Kid's Help Phone: 1-800-668-6868 (Canada)
At www.befrienders.org, you can search for a hotline in your country

Other hotlines:
Family Violence Helpline: 1-800-996-6228
RAINN - The Rape Abuse & Incest National Network: 1-800-656-4673

Online chat when you need help:
https://www.imalive.org/
http://www.crisischat.org/

TTY for Hearing-Impaired:
National Hotline: 1-800-448-1833

You might want to download and read *Suicide: The Forever Decision* by Paul Quinnett. It's a very easy book to read, and offers important information you need before you think more about committing suicide. You can download it at http://www.qprinstitute.com/forever.html.

The website http://www.hisnamewassteven.org/ lists more phone numbers you can call when you need help. This is a website dedicated to Stephen Urry, who committed suicide because he was bullied. Who knows what Stephen could have accomplished in his lifetime if someone had been there to offer him support in his depression?

If you just feel numb

If you find yourself falling into a mood where you feel helpless and hopeless, as if nothing will ever change, your unconscious mind may be bringing up useful information that can help you move past an issue or obstacle that's standing in your way. I call this "the sense of futility," and it's a sign that your mind is trying to help you heal.

There are a number of reasons a child may grow up with a sense of futility, but the primary issue I've discovered is that the sense of futility covers over an immense and terrifying buildup of frustration—a huge well of distress and disappointment at having his needs ignored or belittled time after time after time. If a small child's needs are not met with at least some regularity, there is a tremendous sense of frustration, of powerlessness to get anything that he or she needs. Over time, as the frustration builds up and is repressed over and over again, it becomes too painful to face—and though having a sense of futility is still unpleasant, it's less threatening and painful than tremendous frustration. Futility is a numbing feeling—it offers the option of giving up.

"There can be no transforming of darkness into light and of apathy into movement without emotion."
~ Carl Jung (Swiss psychotherapist, founder of analytical psychology)

Your psyche has hidden all the distress, frustration, and disappointment behind a screen of hopelessness and feelings of futility, because sometimes it's a little easier to cope with life when we're numb.

Imagine that you are standing beside yourself as the "witness" while you think back to when you were younger. Do you remember ever being frustrated? Did you try to get what you wanted, and then discover that someone was always in the way, or that others weren't responsive to your needs? Or did people make promises and then not keep them? Both of those experiences can be very disappointing, especially if they happen frequently. Asking questions like these can help you uncover the original experiences underneath your sense of futility, and clear them away from your psyche. Here's how you do that:

Pick a time when you have at least a half hour to focus. Make a list of all the ways you were frustrated or disappointed in your life, and all the ways you're frustrated or disappointed now. See if you can feel now what you felt like then, when each experience happened—you're calling up that old emotion so it can be released and cleared.

If nothing comes up, try thinking about the place you were in at that time. Was it at home? In your yard or on the street? Were you in your parents' car, or a public place? This can help you call up the old emotion so you can let go of it.

Whatever feelings you have are the feelings you need to express—there are no wrong feelings. The first time I did this, I felt such a huge sense of rage that I didn't know what to do with it. I ended up whapping a yardstick through the air like a sword, saying all the things I would have said—about having my needs ignored and my attempts to explore and learn for myself prevented—if I had been able to talk at that age. I was able to express my frustration and rage in a way that didn't hurt myself or anyone else (or even the yardstick!), and then I was able to move forward and feel better again.

As each emotion comes up, acknowledge and express the old feeling, whether it's anger or sadness or frustration, by doing something like shaking your fists and letting your body move however it wants to move, or crying if you feel like crying. Try to stay in the "witness place" as you do this, keeping a part of yourself separate from the emotion. It may help to pretend there's a part of you standing or sitting right beside yourself as you let the feelings go. Keeping part of yourself as a witness also helps you trust yourself in this process, so you aren't afraid you'll go overboard or lose control. The witness is the part of you that's always able to control your expression of emotion.

Tell yourself (as if you were talking to a child) how sorry you are that the experience happened, that you didn't deserve it, and that things will get better. The more you encourage and support yourself, the more your self-esteem will grow. It feels odd at first, because we're taught to expect our support and encouragement from others, but encouraging yourself is a good way to increase your confidence and self-respect.

Once the emotion has spent itself, go back to pen and paper, and write for a few moments about what you experienced. This helps to get the darker emotions "out of your head" and onto paper. Follow this by writing briefly about how you would like things to be instead. Use your imagination. If you like to create art, for example, imagine yourself joyously painting, showing your paintings in galleries, and having people appreciate and respect your work. Whatever you would like your future to be like, write for a few moments about what that would feel like.

> **"To give vent now and then to his feelings, whether of pleasure or discontent, is a great ease to a man's heart."** ~ Francesco Guicciardini (Italian historian and statesman)

Try to do this at least once a week or more. It will help you let go of your sense of hopelessness and futility, and gain a sense of more control in your life.

One of the most supportive things I found in recovering from my own depression and hopelessness was talking with a therapist. Therapy is very helpful in giving you reality checks—meaning that you can ask, "Is this normal?" about your feelings or someone else's behavior, and have someone help you figure out the answer. Therapy also helps you feel like someone is absolutely on your side.

Once you find the right therapist, you'll discover a relationship that can make you feel empowered, supported, and encouraged, and you'll learn the tools you need to become stronger, more capable, and more confident throughout your life.

Make sure you feel comfortable with a therapist before engaging in a long-term relationship. As with professionals in any field, some therapists are better than others, and there are also differences in the way different people connect in a therapeutic relationship, just as there are in life. Use your intuition—if you feel supported and encouraged by the therapist, it's a good match. If you feel like the person is trying to get you to do things a certain way, or even putting you down, look for someone else. Your school counselor, minister, or doctor can help you find a therapist.

Therapy was the best thing I ever did, absolutely the best thing that ever happened to me. The process totally helped me to discover who I really was underneath all the expectations that other people had dumped on me, and to understand that I was not defective—that it was *the way I had been treated* that made me feel incompetent and hopeless. And it helped me learn how I can cope best with life in a way that suits me. I strongly suggest that you consider the idea—it can make a world of difference in your life to feel like you have someone who is totally on your side.

How to raise your self-esteem and feel more confident

Along with letting go of your painful feelings, there are other things you can do to help yourself feel better. Gaining a sense of confidence may seem impossible to you at the moment, but there are ways to increase your confidence and feel stronger.

> **"The whole theory of the universe is directed unerringly to one single individual— namely to You."**
> ~ Walt Whitman
> (American poet, essayist, and journalist)

Everyone has something that they do well. Are you a good reader? A talented artist? Good at science or math? Maybe children really like you or feel very comfortable with you. Do you have interesting ideas, even if you don't express them? Can you see under the surface of a situation, or know what other people are feeling? Do you love nature or animals, enjoy working with plants or connecting with pets? Even being sensitive is a gift which you can put to a very positive use when you grow up (see the books on being sensitive in the Resource section at the end of the book).

Everyone is different, and everyone has different skills. Unfortunately, our society praises certain skills and talents, and disregards others, but that doesn't mean that the gifts which society belittles (like sensitivity) are worthless. People who love animals can become veterinarians. People who are sensitive might decide to be therapists, writers, healers, actors, or enter any number of other professions. Artists, writers, and musicians can teach along with practicing their art. Young people who love to read about or explore new places can become travel agents or work on cruise ships. Even working jigsaw puzzles exercises parts of your brain that can lead to success in the business world; perhaps in graphic design or magazine or website layout. Whatever you enjoy and are good at can become a profession. It doesn't matter whether it's an "accepted" profession or not—new kinds of businesses and careers are being created every day.

Take a few moments to think about what you do well, and write down a few of your ideas. This list can eventually help you decide what you want to be when you grow up. If you know of any adults who have similar interests, ask if you can talk to them a bit about what they do and how they got where they are.

We're often taught that it's not okay to be proud of ourselves. In some families, modesty is a very important value. Modesty and humility exist on one end of the continuum of self-esteem and confidence, and egotism or arrogance hang out on the other. Arrogant people who think they're so much better than everyone else are usually not especially fun to be around. But having no self-confidence or pride in yourself, even if you're accomplishing a lot, is just as detrimental.

Sometimes young people find themselves in competition with their mothers or fathers—some parents may be subconsciously jealous of their child's youth, attractiveness, intelligence, or opportunities; or they may feel that pride is a sin, and teach the child through their words or behaviors that it's not right to be proud. But it's a natural human behavior to want to feel good about and take pride in what you do well.

It can be difficult to achieve a balance between being too modest and being confident. In some families, feeling pride in what we do is frowned on, and consequently, it's hard to allow ourselves to feel good about our achievements. People can be very confident and filled with pride about their achievements without being egotistical or arrogant. You can feel good about yourself without crossing the line into egotism. In fact, arrogant or egotistical people often don't have real achievements to back up their egotism.

Sometimes we lose our confidence because we feel that others—often our parents—expect us to be able to do certain things or be a certain way. A good example is a father who really wants his son to be a professional athlete—and no matter how much encouragement the father gives, or how much time he spends tossing a baseball or playing basketball with the boy, if the boy is really interested in science or literature or something else, he won't ever be happy or feel confident trying to be a sports star.

> **"Go confidently in the direction of your dreams. Live the life you have imagined."** ~ Henry David Thoreau

If your parents are encouraging you in a certain direction that doesn't feel right for you, try to find a way to tell them that you feel more comfortable doing something else. I know this is very, very hard to do, but you'll feel much more confident if you can focus on what you enjoy doing, on what you feel you do well. Sometimes parents have an internal picture of who they want their child to be, but their image may be based more on what the parent desires than what is right for the child.

If this is true for you, you can try approaching your parents this way: "Mom (or Dad), I appreciate the fact that you really encourage me to do _____. I like having your support. But I'm really not comfortable doing that. I feel much stronger and happier doing _____. Could you support and encourage me for doing that instead?"

If your parents get angry, then you can know for sure that they are trying to satisfy some need within themselves, rather than trying to help you grow in the best way you can. See if you can find support for what you want to do from others instead— teachers, friends, or other adults.

The next step is to grow your skills, to find ways to become even better at what you do well so your confidence increases. Even if you don't have much support for what you want to do, you can support yourself for it. Research careers related to what you want to do, and see if you can find people in those fields to talk with about their experience. Dedicate a certain amount of your time to focusing on what you want to do and doing what you do well.

And remember that no one is good at everything. When we're young, and we're looking at the adults around us, it can seem as if they know how to do everything, and do it well. They've had years and years of experience to help them learn how to do things. Competence comes from practice—beginning with trial and error, finding out what works and what doesn't. No adult is born knowing how to do things well; we all make mistakes in the process of learning.

At your age, you're in one of the most difficult stages of life—the time when you're learning how you as an individual can best cope with the world. What works for you may not be what other people think is right, but your life will be much more fulfilling if you choose your own way of doing things instead of following someone else's way or doing what society determines "should" be best for you. Some of the most successful businesses in the world have been created by people who lived outside the "norm," and believed so much in their intuition and instincts that they didn't let others stop them from what they knew in their hearts they wanted to do.

Part 3 – Coping with Bullies

Tips for coping with bullies

★ ★ ★ ★ ★ ★ ★ ★ ★ ★ ★
**"I don't have to attend
every argument I'm
invited to."**
~ Author Unknown
★ ★ ★ ★ ★ ★ ★ ★ ★ ★ ★

Now that you know a little bit about why kids become bullies, it may be easier for you to cope with being bullied. This section will give you some ideas for dealing with bullies. If you practice these tactics in your mind before you get into a situation with a bully, it will be easier for you to use them when a bully is right in front of you. Choose the one that appeals most to you, and practice using it in your mind several times a day.

1. When you react to a bully with anger, frustration, or fear, you are adding fuel to the fire. Bullies torment people in order to feel stronger inside, and getting a big reaction or seeing someone become emotional because of what they do makes them feel stronger. They don't really want to hurt you; they just want to win. On a deep psychological level, they may even be trying to get back at someone else who is hurting them by putting you down.

So even if it's upsetting, don't give them a big reaction. Act like you don't care. You can just walk away, or even say, "So what?" Don't take what the bully says personally, because that causes you to lose your center, your sense of self.

By not reacting, you are winning the game the bully is playing, because they don't get what they want, and you are still in charge of yourself.

2. If it's not frightening, finding a way to chuckle at the situation may defuse it.

3. If someone tries to bully you with a rumor, like "You're really stupid," ask them, "Do you really believe that?" If they say yes, you can say, "Well, that's your opinion. Everyone has different opinions."

4. Many bullies will be put off if you stop where you are, give them a look, and say clearly and assertively, "Excuse me?"

5. If they push you or bump into you, just walk away. Remember that by not reacting, you deflate the excitement they hope to get from bullying you.

6. You can make believe you don't hear them, or say, "What?"

7. You can ignore a bully and just go right back to what you were doing. If they don't stop, you can say, "Excuse me, I need to use the restroom," and leave.

8. If you feel like the bully is draining your energy or "pulling on you" in any way, you can usually stop this by folding your arms across your stomach, standing with your feet farther apart, and pulling your energy back toward yourself. This strengthens your own energy field and can help you feel more protected. Many bullies are what some people call "psychic vampires"— they try to suck up your energy by pretending they're more powerful. Unless this has happened to you, you may not believe it, but it does occur, particularly with sensitive people. Some sensitive people even pick up on others' emotions. Do some reading about subtle energy fields (see the Resources section), auras, and personal energy, and experiment with different ways of protecting your energy field.

9. Use a communication technique called "Respond, don't react," which can help you hold on to a sense of your own power. Keep your cool if someone is trying to bully you. Bullies enjoy watching their victims fly into a rage or turn red in embarrassment, and if you just stand and watch, calmly and rationally, they may run out of steam. Stand back from yourself (like when you're working with the witness) and pretend you're watching the opening scene of a film. Let the bully tease you without interrupting, and the person will eventually get tired and start wondering what's going on. If you can smile a little in the midst of it, so much the better—the bully will think you know a secret about him or her.

> "There is nothing more galling to angry people than the coolness of those on whom they wish to vent their spleen."
> ~ Alexandre Dumas (French writer)

When the bully stops talking, reply calmly and rationally to let her know you're still in command of yourself. Your response might be something like, "I know I'm tall, and I have many other wonderful qualities, too." In my case, if I had thought to respond to "Metal Mouth" with "And my teeth will look absolutely great in about two years," I would've been way ahead of the game.

Spend some time thinking of an appropriate reply beforehand, so you're prepared when the bully strikes again. Deliver your response in a calm, clear voice, and then turn and walk away with your dignity intact. Remember that posture also shows others how you feel about yourself: if you slouch, bullies will think you're an easy target. If you walk with your shoulders wide and your head up, you project a sense of pride and strength that's not as easy to cut down.

You can practice some of these tactics in your mind while you're walking or riding a bus or taking a shower. Imagine that a bully has just stepped in front of you—imagine their words or gestures, and remind yourself that you're not going to take anything personally, that you can just keep your cool and not get involved in the incident. Pick one of the tactics above to rehearse first, and run through a scene in your mind several times using that tactic. Then see yourself walking away feeling strong and confident. Pick another tactic and do the same with that one. Practice as often as you can, so that the tactics come to mind quickly if you run into a bully.

What to do if a teacher or coach is bullying you

As we saw in the section on bullying by parents, adults can be bullies, too. If a teacher or coach is bullying you or someone else, his behavior is just as wrong as the behavior of a student who bullies others, and should be called to the attention of the principal and school officials. If this is happening to you, try to get a friend to go with you to verify your claim when you speak to the principal. Be sure to use the word "bullying" when you're talking about the adult's behavior, and try to have specific examples ready to mention.

If you're acting on behalf of someone else, you might think about making a written statement of the event, and having several people who were present sign it if you can. I suggest not mentioning the name of the bullying victim, so he can maintain a sense of privacy—just call attention to the teacher's or coach's behavior.

Some schools have "drop boxes" where you can write a note about a situation where you or someone else has been bullied. If you don't want to speak to the principal face to face, you can leave a note in a drop box, or even mail it anonymously to the principal's attention at the school.

It's scary sometimes to speak up against people who hurt us— but it's the right thing to do. If we don't ask for help, the bullying will just continue, and may even get worse. Teachers and coaches sometimes think that by pushing their students, they're encouraging them to perform better. But there's a difference between "tough love," or encouraging someone to really challenge themselves, and bullying. In this case, you can pretty much trust your feelings: if the person's behavior makes you want to try harder, get stronger or smarter, and become better at what you're doing, then it's encouragement. If the behavior makes you feel small and unimportant, then it's not encouragement, it's most likely bullying.

"Great spirits have always encountered violent opposition from mediocre minds." ~ Albert Einstein

When a friend becomes a bully

Sometimes friends seem to turn on us, and we don't know why. This can be very confusing, and make you feel as if you can't trust anyone. There may be a particular reason your friend has changed, and if you can find out what it is, the experience may be less hurtful.

Since many people are not taught that it's okay to feel proud of who they are, sometimes young people help themselves feel better by zeroing in on someone else's unusual traits rather than emphasizing their own positive qualities. For whatever reason, they can't feel confident about themselves, so they try to make others feel smaller.

If a friend has turned on you and started bullying you, and you like that friend well enough to see if you can work the problem out, try to have a conversation with the person in private. Ask the person what's going on, and explain how you feel about it. Be specific and point out examples of the behavior that's been hurting you. It's not a good idea to do this in front of other people, because you'll be putting your friend on the defensive, and that might make the situation worse. Try to find a private place when you both have a little time, so you can explain your feelings.

Using "I" language is less threatening to a listener in this kind of situation, which means stating everything from your own point of view: "I felt hurt when you did this," instead of "You hurt me when you did this"; or "I don't understand why this is happening" rather than "What are you doing this for?" Prepare for the discussion ahead of time by writing your thoughts down, so you have set phrases that are easy to remember when you're facing the person who's been hurting you, and practice the phrases you want to use.

Sometimes friendships can be restored after one person hurts another; sometimes they can't. Your intuition will probably tell you what's right for any situation, and again, remember to not take anything personally. Your friend probably changed because of some problem she's having, not because of who you are. Perhaps your friend is having trouble at home, or in another relationship, or even just going through a difficult period, having doubts about herself.

Remember that you can't control how others behave, but you can control your inner world and your own response to the situation. The less you let the bully's words and actions into your energy field, the less frustrated and hurt you'll feel. And remember that bullying won't go on forever. Eventually, the school year will end, and eventually you'll graduate and either go to college or out into the world, where you'll have the opportunity to interact with many, many new people.

If one of your friends is bullying someone else, don't jump on the bandwagon and add your own power to the bully's arsenal. You may not know what it feels like to be ganged up on, but maybe you can imagine how awful it is. People sometimes don't realize how deeply being bullied can affect a girl or boy until that person commits suicide, and then it's too late.

If you're comfortable defending the victim—saying something like, "Hey, that's not a nice thing to say"—that is admirable behavior. But you might be afraid that the bully will turn on you if you do that, so it's okay not to. You can certainly stand back from the situation and not participate, or even act as if it's the most uninteresting thing in the world. You can also tell a teacher or school counselor or nurse about it so that you're not getting involved personally in the situation.

Cyberbullying

Although it takes place within a social media situation, cyberbullying has the same causes as the bullying that happens at school, and it feels pretty much the same. Just like bullying in person, it makes you feel negative and doubt yourself.

> **"Never be bullied into silence. Never allow yourself to be made a victim. Accept no one's definition of your life, but define yourself."**
> ~ Oliver Wendell Holmes (American physician, poet, writer, humorist and Harvard professor)

The difference is that with cyberbullying, lots of people—some of whom may not even know you—can join in just by typing a few words. In the same way that bullies at school like to put others down in order to feel stronger, some people go online and cyberbully as a way of venting their anger at someone else or another situation.

There's also a certain "distance" on the web that makes people feel even more comfortable joining in to bully someone, almost as if it's a virtual game, with characters instead of real people. The cyberbully's friends (who may be your friends) sometimes join in just because they don't want to become targets themselves. They align themselves with the bully so that the bully doesn't turn on them next. They may not really want to participate; they're just trying to keep themselves safe. So it becomes a game, with people taking sides and trying to get more and more people on their side. The more people someone can get on their side, the more powerful they feel—but that power is meaningless, because it's not a true power that comes from achieving goals or creating value in the world.

The most important thing to remember is something that bears repeating: you don't have to take the bullying personally. You don't have to believe anything that is written about you. A cyberbully is just looking for someone to make fun of. The fact that a person needs to cyberbully shows how small he feels inside.

Here are some things you can do to prevent cyberbullying, and to stop it if someone is bullying you on the web:

1. Keep your information private. Don't give out passwords or other information.

2. Be careful about who you invite to Friend you on Facebook.

3. Don't use applications on social networking sites that allow people to post anonymously on your page.

4. If you're targeted by a cyberbully, your first reaction will probably be very emotional. Before you do anything, take five minutes to calm down, acknowledge your feelings, and remind yourself that you're in a safe place. Remember that they're just looking for someone to pick on, and you happened to be the "target of the day."

5. You can ignore a cyberbully, just as you can ignore a real bully. If you react or try to defend yourself, you'll probably just provoke the cyberbully to do more. Close your browser or go to another website.

6. Block the cyberbully on your accounts, or limit all communications to anyone on your Friend list who is cyberbullying you. Don't read the messages you're blocking—they will only add to your upset.

7. Tell someone you trust, so that you can get help coping with the situation. Tell your parents, and talk with them about whether or not to inform the police.

8. Don't delete the messages. If the cyberbullying continues, you may need proof that it happened.

9. Deactivate social networking accounts and change your email address and cell phone numbers if the bullying persists.

10. Report it to the website. A cyberbully's accounts can be blocked if they are reported often by different people.

11. Don't retaliate or try to get even with them—you may find yourself in an even worse position.

12. Don't try to defuse the situation by placating the bully. This is a reaction—and any kind of response can fuel the fire.

Take the same steps you would take if someone is bullying you at school: report the bullying, ask for help, and use the four-step plan to let go of your feelings.

Part 4 – For Bullies: If you feel so bad that you just want to hurt someone

Sometimes we get so mad that we just want to lash out at someone. Our feelings can be so overwhelming that we don't know what to do with them, and we think that if we hurt someone else or put them down, we'll feel better. We might feel better for awhile when we see how we can make someone else react the way we want them to, but then later we go back to feeling the anger we felt before, and we want to lash out again.

Sometimes someone is hurting us, and we want to make other people hurt as much as we're hurting. We may have never learned that there are other, better ways besides lashing out at other people to deal with hurts and anger. But there are.

If you just started reading here, go back to the Four-Step Plan and look at the section on expressing anger. There are lots of ways to express anger in a healthy way, which means expressing it without hurting someone else or yourself. You can whack a bed with a plastic bat, throw rocks in a river or pond, or go for a walk or work out at the gym—anything that gets your body moving will help you to let go of your anger and pain. And there are lots of ways to help yourself feel better if you're sad or hurting inside, and lots of ways to get good attention when you need it. You might want to start at the beginning of the book and read about what makes us sad and angry.

One of the problems with school is that kids have to sit for hours at a time, and focus on things they may not really want to focus on. This is very frustrating! Having only an hour or two of physical activity where you can run or move around or play sports isn't enough activity for everyone. Some people need more physical activity than others. If you've never tried sports or some other kind of physical activity after school, you might want to give it a try and see if it makes you feel better.

"Holding on to anger is like grasping a hot coal with the intent of throwing it at someone else; you are the one who gets burned." ~ Buddha

Sometimes you might want to hurt other kids because someone at home or somewhere else is hurting you. You want to retaliate, to hit back, but you can't hit back at the person who's hurting you or putting you down, so you find someone smaller or weaker to hit back at. It's a normal reaction to want to hit back when you've been hurt or humiliated, but *it's not ever appropriate to hit back at someone who's not hurting you.*

If someone is hurting or humiliating you, see the section on "How to Ask for Help." If the first person you ask doesn't help, keep asking until you find someone who will. It's not ever right for parents or other adults to hurt or humiliate kids, and you need to get support in coping with this kind of problem. If you make it clear to the person you ask that you don't want your parents to know you're asking for help, and that you just want some support in coping with the problem, most people will honor your wishes, and your parents won't have to know.

If someone in your family is hurting you, their behavior is wrong. You may love this person (you can love the *person* and still know that their *behavior* is wrong), but the way they're behaving is inappropriate. Love is not supposed to hurt. Read the section "When Parents Are Bullies."

> **"Whatever is begun in anger ends in shame."**
> ~ Benjamin Franklin

Sometimes bullying is a "learned behavior"—maybe you're just copying what someone else does. If you see someone who seems very powerful bullying someone else, you might think that bullying is what makes them powerful. But it doesn't work that way. Many adults who bully others—including their kids—do it because they feel like little children inside, and they're using the behavior of bullying to try to feel more important, bigger. They're looking for attention, but they don't know of any positive ways to get it, so they bully others. Parents bullying their children are just as wrong as kids bullying other kids.

There are steps you can take to help yourself feel better, so you don't want so badly to hurt someone else. The first step is to understand the feelings you have inside—they're probably a result of your being hurt, maybe over and over, as you've been growing up. So the first thing to do is to go back to the Four-Step Plan, find the emotion you feel the most of, and start expressing it using the suggestions under that emotion. If you have a lot of different feelings, pick the one that's bothering you the most, and start there. It takes some time, but generally people feel better pretty quickly once they start expressing their feelings.

The next step for you is to find other ways besides bullying to feel stronger and more powerful. Here are some suggestions to try:

1. Some people like to lift weights to feel stronger, or practice some form of exercise that makes their body feel stronger.

2. Deep breathing, or practicing a martial art like Tai Chi or Karate, or Qi Gong, can help you feel stronger. Martial arts help you connect with the power and strength inside of you, and Qi Gong teaches you how to gather in the life force energy that exists all around us to create a healthier, stronger body.

3. Even jumping up and down for a few moments can give you a feeling of more power. As your body moves, your blood circulates and your brain gets going. This also helps you feel more positive.

4. Some people help others in order to feel stronger. By providing a service to others who are in need, we realize that we have more strength than we thought.

The last step in feeling better is to learn new ways to get others to help you get what you want. The first thing to try is asking: "Can you help me with this?" Or "Can I ask what you think about something?"

In spite of what you may have learned, asking is not a sign of weakness; it's a sign of wanting to know more, to do better, to learn and become more confident about life and the world. You may have learned as a child that asking didn't get you anywhere, because some people are not good at responding to requests. But if you keep trying, you'll find people that will help you get what you want.

"What you are seeking is also seeking you." ~ Rumi (13th century Persian poet)

Another way to get what you want is to help others get what they want. In some families, everyone is focused on meeting their own needs, rather than helping everyone to get what they want, and you may have thought that's how life works. But offering to help someone else to get what they want makes it easier to ask for what you want. When people work together rather than against each other, it's more likely that everyone can get their needs met. If your family is one of those where everyone focuses on their own needs, it might be better to find people outside of your family who you can help—people who would be willing to help you in return.

★ ★

"The finest thing in the world is knowing how to belong to oneself." ~ Michel de Montaigne, *Of Solitude* (French Renaissance writer)

★ ★

Seeing a therapist or school counselor can be very helpful in learning new ways to get what you want, and in learning how to feel in charge of your life. A therapist can give you tools that will help you succeed and feel more confident, and can give you the support you need to create new goals so you don't need to hurt others in order to feel better.

A final note: If you feel like you truly can't control your actions, it's very important to ask for help. Sometimes feelings of frustration can be related to food allergies, or chemical imbalances, or other problems that can easily be remedied. But you won't know if you don't ask! Next time you see your doctor, ask to speak privately with him or her. Explain how you feel, and ask if there are any options for helping you feel better.

What's most important is for you to feel good about yourself and your life, and though it may take some time, it's absolutely possible. I know—I've been in some very bad places in my life, and in asking for help I've been able to move beyond the problems and learn how to get more of what I want. You can, too.

Part 5 – Interviews: How to Recover from Bullying

Michelle Baker, Director of Education, Blaze My Trail Youth Program

Ms. Baker is a visual and performing artist, writer, and Director of the Blaze My Trail Youth Program. In this interview, she explains how she felt as a victim of abuse, how she turned her life around, and what she suggests for young people who have been victimized by bullies.

> **"Emotional bullying is often likened to taking hostages. It is well-documented that the effects of psychological abuse...are longer-lasting than those of outright physical violence."**
> ~ Michelle Baker

Q: What form of emotional abuse or bullying did you experience in your early life?

A: The bullying I remember most was from my mother, both physical and psychological, and from my community because they did not intervene on my behalf, even when I turned to them for help.

Q: How did it make you feel (mentally, physically, emotionally, and spiritually)?

A: As a young girl, I was very withdrawn, and I turned to drawing and writing stories for my escape and sanctuary. I always felt like an outsider, never understanding why other children were so happy and able to run around, laugh and shout out loud. I aimed to be as quiet as possible because I was afraid of drawing attention to myself.

In my teenage years, I did a "180." Though I still felt like an outsider, I capitalized on that by turning to drugs and very risky behavior in the desperate hope of getting attention.

As a consequence, I have struggled with feelings of shame and unworthiness in my adult life.

Q: Were there external circumstances, such as low grades or lack of friendships that you believe were a result of the bullying?

A: As a result of the bullying, I was very introverted, and did not believe I was worthy of being a part of anything. As a young child, I was shy. As a teen, I engaged in behaviors that alienated me even more. My grades were very good until ninth grade, when I went from being a straight-A student to having C's and D's. I brought my grades back up slowly, making honors lists again as a senior, but my self-esteem was severely compromised. During that last year of high school, I made new friendships outside of the drug culture I had been a part of, and aimed to make safer social choices.

Q: Did you have any outlets for your emotions as a child?

A: My grandmother was very tender. She held me while I cried, and protected my quiet time, letting me draw and color. At age 12, that relationship changed as my mother began to separate from needing her family so much. I turned then to spirituality, but also became very depressed. During that time, my mother's physical and emotional violence escalated. My grandparents were no longer a buffer for my mother or me as she began to separate from them and embark on her own journey of psychological reconciliation.

I cultivated a very real and private spirituality—even in my rebellious teenage years. After school, I would go for bike rides, stop at a church, and go inside. I'd sit in a pew by myself, and pray and cry. In fact, most of my "ride" was spent in a church just a few minutes away from my house. I'd spend about an hour there, and then return home. It was the only place I felt safe and sure not to be disturbed.

> "I have continued to give my voice freedom...creatively and professionally. This is a work in constant progress, but one I am dedicated to."
> ~ Michelle Baker

When I was 15, I turned to drugs, failing school, and risky sexual behavior as a means to "vent" my emotions because I had no other way to let go of them. Thankfully, I kept journals starting from the age of 12, and believe my dedication to writing and cultivating an inner spiritual life kept me choosing to stay alive.

Q: Were there any people in your life who supported your strengths and encouraged your accomplishments? If so, can you describe your relationship with them, and the effect of their positive attention on you and your feelings?

A: I had two teachers in my life who supported my strengths and encouraged my accomplishments. My seventh-grade English teacher was quite dynamic and innovative. He introduced his class to the Beat poets and the music of the 60s. He encouraged us to look beyond what was written or spoken, and consider a deeper meaning. I flourished in that class, and he recognized that.

Then, my Latin teacher from ninth through twelfth grades saw right through my rebellious veneer. He confronted my mother, and he confronted me and my drug use. He kept telling me the best rebellion was that of applying oneself in the face of adversity. He was a gay man who taught at very conservative prep school. He had graduated from high school when he was 16, and graduated from college by the age of 19 in a time when sexual orientation was never talked about. But he also never denied his orientation. He simply lived in a way that could not be questioned because he excelled...quite possibly over-compensating, but nevertheless, letting his brilliance shine unapologetically, and always graciously. He knew I was suicidal, and he unceasingly pointed towards the "exit" of turning 18 and finally being free to live on my own. He always invited me to live more fully by excelling in school and showing me how that opens doors to so many opportunities. I am forever grateful to him for that.

Q: Were you able to ask for help in recovering from the abuse and bullying?

A: As a child, I asked twice, and I was reprimanded both times. I kept quiet until my early 30s, and then went into therapy for trauma for a solid seven years. I have since returned for grief work.

Q: What steps did you take to recover?

A: I'd say that my first taste of recovery was going to school for expressive arts therapy at Tamalpa Institute in the Bay Area. Influenced by the work of Fritz Perls, it was there that I first allowed myself to create artwork directly addressing my history of abuse. It was fantastically liberating! My artwork flourished. And from that moment on, I have continued to give my voice freedom...creatively and professionally. This is a work in constant progress, but one I am dedicated to.

Q: How did you try to increase your confidence, your feeling of safety in the world, and your ability to trust other people?

A: By moving away from my hometown, I gave myself the chance to meet new people, who didn't know my family and didn't have any particular allegiance to their reputation. I surrounded myself with people who were and are devoted to healing and living a whole-hearted life, whether they suffered from abuse and bullying or not.

I am still working on safety in the world. I tend to walk around as if I have an armored plate on my chest. People perceive me as not needing anyone or anything. It is an attitude of defense that I

> **"Know with all your heart that there is help, and that your story can help someone else."**
> ~ Michelle Baker

learned when I was very young, and one I am working on softening, because I do very much need and enjoy friendship and community.

As for trusting people, I have an amazing number of good people in my life. For the most part, I attract people with clear boundaries. This isn't always the case, obviously, but my positive experiences as an adult far outweigh my negative experiences.

Q: In your mind, what would be the most important thing to say to a young person who is being bullied or abused?

A: Tell someone, and tell someone who believes you. Tell someone who believes you and who is willing to help you. Learn the difference between truly helpful actions and intentions, and manipulative or exploitative ones. Find an outlet that is creative and safe. If you feel like harming yourself or others, put that into art or writing, and seek counseling to help you learn how to manage those very difficult and very real feelings and thoughts.

Know with all your heart that there is help, and that your story can help someone else. Sometimes we might not find the people who help us right away; but know that your experience might very well be the thing another person needs to hear in order to choose to live. This, I believe, is the call to all victims, and to all bullies who have sought professional help and have taken action to transform themselves.

Only you know when your safety depends on silence, but always ask for help...even if you have to whisper for it. My favorite saying happens to be a title of a book, *Courage Doesn't Always Roar* (by Mary Anne Radmacher). And remember, one day, your story, your art, your voice, your life just might be exactly what another person needs in order to choose life.

Q: Anything else you'd like to say?

A: Emotional bullying is often likened to being held hostage. It is well-documented that the effects of psychological abuse and the psychological repercussions of physical abuse are longer-lasting than those of outright physical violence. While the broken or injured body can heal fairly rapidly on its own and with medical intervention, the broken or injured emotional body takes much longer, and in some instances is impossible to heal on its own. Healing the emotional body takes commitment, and is fostered with the help of professionals and supportive friends and family. Always seek help. By allowing people to help, we rebuild trust, healthy communities, and learn to love ourselves and others again.

And finally, always remember, you are not alone. There is always someone who can and will relate to your situation and help you.

~

Many thanks to Michelle for sharing her experience!

Amy Wood, Psy.D., inspirational speaker
and author of "Life Your Way"

Ms. Wood is a speaker, coach, and author of *Life Your Way*, a very inspirational book which helps readers set specific goals and expectations for achieving success. In this interview, she offers suggestions for forging ahead and acting assertively, even if you don't feel that way inside, and provides tips for coping with bullying.

Q: How did being bullied make you feel (mentally, physically, emotionally, and spiritually)?

A: Bullying made me feel inadequate, afraid to speak up, stupid, unattractive, left out, depressed, and anxious. Also, I was sensitive and analytical, and I internalized a lot of stuff—took it personally—and that made me feel responsible for the bullying. So I went deeper into myself in a blaming way, rather than fighting back or reaching out for help.

• • • • • • •

"I realized when I graduated from college that I was responsible for changing my life by becoming more assertive, and that put me on a new path that I've never wavered from."
~ Amy Wood

• • • • • • •

Q: Were there external circumstances, such as low grades or lack of friendships that you believe were a result of the bullying?

A: I was smaller than most kids and very shy, and I think I was an easy target for these reasons. Also, I was an American living in Canada—not common in the 70s, and kids—and often their parents—thought I was almost like an alien from another land.

Q: Did you have any outlets for your emotions as a child?

A: Yes. I always had a few really solid friends and many close family members. We had great fun together, and I was encouraged by my parents to let loose and be active and creative. But my parents did not invite my expression of emotional distress. If I expressed any unhappiness, they would tell me I should stop complaining and be grateful because other children had it worse than me, and some were starving.

> "My parents had no idea that I was bullied because I never told them." ~ Amy Wood

Q: Were there any people in your life who supported your strengths and encouraged your accomplishments? If so, can you describe your relationship with them, and the effect of their positive attention on you and your feelings?

A: My parents and all my adult relatives supported my strengths and encouraged my accomplishments, but my parents had too much confidence in me. I was the oldest, and very responsible and smart, so they didn't think I needed any help or structure, which of course I desperately needed.

Q: Were you able to ask for help in recovering from bullying?

A: When I was growing up, it wasn't called bullying. It wasn't recognized as a problem to be addressed. I just figured that because I got picked on a lot as a kid, I deserved it in some way—especially because my teachers never did anything about it. My parents had no idea that I was bullied because I never told them—I just thought it was normal for small, shy kids (or overweight kids or otherwise unpopular kids) like me to be treated badly.

Q: What steps did you take to recover?

A: The bullying stopped when my family moved from Ottawa to Florida the summer before I started tenth grade. All the kids at my new school loved me because I was a novelty, coming from Canada, and that's when I began to realize that what I had experienced the years before was not normal, and was in fact bullying. Even though the bullying stopped in tenth grade, the impact of it kept me feeling insecure and inadequate, anxious and depressed for years. Sometimes I still feel that impact, but my life is much more positive now.

I realized when I graduated from college that I was responsible for changing my life by becoming more assertive, and that put me on a new path that I've never wavered from. I've had therapy a few times and that has helped, but my recovery has come mostly from being fully accountable for my life and my personal and professional growth, and keeping myself out of negative relationships, toxic job environments, and the like.

Q: How did you try to increase your confidence, your feeling of safety in the world, and your ability to trust other people?

A: I just forged ahead despite my inner belief—developed in early childhood—that I was a loser. I started acting assertive, and did all sorts of things to become more confident: I was very ambitious in my career, took acting classes, joined various groups, and reached out to make friends, and since then I have felt much safer in the world, way more trusting of others, and increasingly fulfilled and happy.

> **"Bullies are apt to lose interest if they don't have the thrill of a reaction."**
> ~ Amy Wood

Q: In your mind, what would be the most important thing to say to a young person who is being bullied?

A: The most important message to give young people being bullied is that it is wrong and they don't have to put up with it. Bullied kids should be taught to be assertive, and taught that they matter. Most importantly, they should be told that they will never be able to control the behavior of others, but that they can control their own inner world, their responses, and the development of their own character.

Q: Do you have any thoughts on what teachers and parents can do to stop bullying in our schools?

A: The answer is to have a no-tolerance rule for bullying, just like we have with sexual harassment and hostile work environments. Bullying should never be acceptable. Beyond a no-tolerance attitude, kids should be taught that it's cool to be nice to each other despite differences, and kids who are bullying because they are being mistreated at home should be given the support they need. Thank goodness, teachers and counselors now know how to recognize the signs, and should step forward to help when they do.

Q: Why do you think kids bully other kids?

A: Most kids bully other kids because they are being neglected, bullied, or otherwise mistreated at home. The bigger reason kids bully, though, is that peer acceptance and being "cool" is the top priority for most kids, and one way to gain acceptance with the popular kids is to prove you're not a loser by making fun of kids who are classified as losers.

Q: What's the first thing you'd say to a kid who came to you and said they were being bullied?

A: I'd tell that kid that bullying should never be tolerated, and I'd ask them to tell me their story. Then I'd refer them to a counselor, and report the bully or bullies.

Q: What could someone do to stop a bully from harassing them?

A: Ignore them and walk away. Bullies are apt to lose interest if they don't have the thrill of a reaction. If the bullying persists or escalates, the next step would be to report the bully to an appropriate authority.

Q: Do you have any suggestions to help kids who have been victims of bullying increase their self-esteem?

A: Do what I did. Take smart risks to become confident. Get therapy. Keep developing personally and professionally. Learn to recognize toxic and abusive behavior and refuse to put up with it.

~

Many thanks to Amy for sharing her thoughts and insights!

Kathi Dezenzo, Clinical Social Worker

Ms. Dezenzo is a clinical social worker and mother of two boys. In her counseling practice, she works with adults who experienced bullying when they were young, to help them recover from the trauma. She says, "If you've been bullied, the most important thing to know is that you are not at fault for what happened, and that you're entitled to all of your feelings. The adults in your life should have protected you. You need to find a way to express your feelings, to talk about what happened to you and how it made you feel."

"You don't have to listen to what anyone else says, and you don't have to care what they think."
~ Kathi Dezenzo

★ ★ ★ ★ ★ ★ ★ ★ ★ ★ ★

She also makes another very important point: "Don't internalize the experience of being humiliated and criticized. In other words, don't take the bully's words as truth about who you are, and don't beat yourself up in the same way a bully does. You don't have to buy into what others say about you—you can choose instead to focus on your strengths, values and goals, while accepting yourself on your own terms."

Sometimes, the more you're living up to your potential and moving forward in your life, the more some people want to put you down, because it makes them uncomfortable with themselves. "When you stand out from the crowd, it can threaten people," Ms. Dezenzo says. "But you can be different without being 'less-than' someone else. Figure out who you are and what you want, and don't let anyone tell you how to live your life. You don't have to listen to what anyone else says, and you don't have to care what they think. What's most important is choosing what *you* want to do with your life."

Ms. Dezenzo emphasizes that many of the bullied and abused clients she's worked with are intelligent and attractive, and not stereotypical "outcasts"—they are people with many wonderful qualities and abilities. Jealousy can cause people who feel "less-than" to criticize and belittle those who seem to be brighter, more capable, more attractive.

If you've come up with a wonderful, unique idea, or are expressing yourself in a very unique way, Ms. Dezenzo suggests that others may see you as a threat, especially if you're smart and attractive. "If you try new things that are outside of the social 'norms,' it can call attention to you and make others feel like they're not good enough," Ms. Dezenzo advises. "That's their problem, not yours. It's very important to grow and expand and explore, and to do things in your own way—that's how we create our lives the way we want them to be.

"The bullying won't go on forever. If you've never had an experience like this before, it may help to know that it will end, and life will get better." Ms. Dezenzo strongly believes that "'You will recover' is true, even if you can't feel that right now. Going to college or being out in the workforce can offer new opportunities with a wider range of people you'll come in contact with, and a greater likelihood of finding people who are more open-minded and tolerant."

"Some people develop learned helplessness from being the repetitive target of bullying, because being bullied damages your self-esteem and make it difficult for you to see yourself as capable and effective," Ms. Dezenzo says. Learned helplessness means giving up on trying to make things better even though there might be actions we could take to improve situations, and it usually results from our experience with uncontrollable events.

"Often, learned helplessness begins in childhood for those who suffered neglect and abuse, or who witnessed a parent showing signs of this condition. Learned helplessness occurs when you try and try over a period of time to get someone to leave you alone, but they won't, so you begin to feel helpless in the situation, and that feeling of helplessness can bleed over into the rest of your life, even if you are competent in many other areas."

> "Therapy can help you manage stress, sadness, anger, and fear, and can give you tools for standing up to bullies."
> ~ Kathi Dezenzo

Learned helplessness can lead to hopelessness and depression—a feeling that you have no power. But you do. Ms. Dezenzo reiterates, "You may feel you can't do anything about being bullied. But you have all kinds of options.

"You need to recognize what happened, talk about it, and learn to set boundaries. And ask for help. Therapy can help you manage stress, sadness, anger, and fear, and can give you tools for standing up to bullies."

~

Many thanks to Ms. Dezenzo for sharing her expertise and insights! Working with a therapist on your own can be one of the best tools you have for recovering from being bullied.

NOTE:

Some researchers believe that learned helplessness may be prevented or reversed by learning to view situations in a more positive way, using language such as "I can do this," or "Time will change things, probably for the better." Many people can achieve this by themselves with a little practice, perseverance and patience, and there are all kinds of resources on the net for overcoming learned helplessness and thinking more positively (also see the Resources section).

Matt Posner, Author of "School of the Ages" and New York City Teacher

Matt Posner is the author of the *School of the Ages* book series for teens, which revolves around a magic school in New York, and is co-author (with Jess C. Scott) of *Teen Guide to Sex and Relationships*, an advice book for young people written from the point of view of older friends. He teaches English in New York City. In this interview, he writes from a place of experience working with young people every day at school, and speaks about his own experience with being bullied.

Q: As a teacher, you must have had ample opportunities to observe the interaction between kids in school. Why do you think kids bully other kids?

A: Children are not generally born with empathy. It's a skill that has to be learned, that parents and other adults have to teach. The nature of children, and the nature of many adults, too, is to define themselves as members of a group and to reject those outside the group. It's a form of tribal behavior left over from our biological past. So when a young child bullies, it's a form of affirming strength and identity by attacking a mysterious Other.

Later in life, a bully is made in the way your book so poignantly identifies: being bullied at home, the child absorbs the behavior as a life strategy. A role model at home does it, so on a subconscious level, it equates to normality. Also, the bad feelings of shame and weakness that come from being bullied can be acted out— not expressed, but acted out—by selecting a weaker target to whom the feelings may be transferred.

> **"Find people who like things you like, and hang out with them. The sting of being bullied won't ever vanish, but it can be overwhelmed with positive feelings from being part of things."** ~ Matt Posner

Q: What's the first thing you'd say to a kid who came to you and said they were being bullied?

A: My goal would be to ask questions and listen and get the full details. There isn't a generic answer to such situations. I need to understand the dynamic between the two kids. I need to get into the heads of both of them. The bully is also a victim.

Q: What could someone do to stop a bully from harassing them?

A: I think the best way to get rid of a bully is to have friends and to be busy. I don't mean friends who go away when the bully approaches, nor do I mean friends who will fight the bully for you, but rather friends who are just there and obviously like you so that you don't seem like an easy target. Being busy also makes you not look like a target. If you are involved in school activities, or sports, or stuff in the community, if you are fully engaged in the world, you will grow in confidence and security so that you don't feel like the sort of person who gets bullied. From there, standing up for yourself comes next.

> Standing up for yourself doesn't necessarily mean physically fighting back. It can simply be a matter of asserting your confidence and your personality."
> ~ Matt Posner

Bullying involves two participants. How you react to the bully determines whether the bullying works. If you are obviously upset, if you carry yourself like a victim, the bully gets satisfaction and returns for more. If your reaction does not feed that pleasure—if you act like the bullying is strange or is not happening—then the bully may not get the emotional release desired, and will probably move on.

Standing up for yourself doesn't necessarily mean physically fighting back. It can simply be a matter of asserting your confidence and your personality.

Q: Do you have any suggestions to help kids who have been victims of bullying increase their self-esteem?

A: It's what I said before: be busy. Join clubs and teams in school; go to community events outside school. Find people who like things you like and hang out with them. The sting of being bullied won't ever vanish, but it can be overwhelmed with positive feelings from being part of things.

Q: What do you think is behind the occurrences of school violence, such as the Sandy Hook tragedy?

A: I just did a unit on this in my school, so I have been studying and thinking about it. I believe school shootings are caused ultimately by brain damage, whether congenital or caused by injury. All the factors of loneliness and social isolation, being victims of bullying, ready availability of guns, depression and despair, and so on, all would be more likely to point to suicide than homicide. To kill without remorse, in a methodical and systematic way, is the product of some sort of brain damage that removes capacity for compassion. Antisocial personality disorder (psychopathy, sociopathy), schizophrenia, psychosis, and severe depression are all the result of organic problems.

So while bullying has played a part in a lot of school shooting cases, it isn't a universal factor, and I don't think it is on a list of causes so much as it is on a list of events that can trigger a potential for violence that certain individuals have. Children who are severely bullied tend to kill themselves.

Q: Can you think of any ways to help kids who want to commit suicide as a result of bullying?

A: This is a matter for a mental health professional to comment on, but as a layman, I can only say what I've said already: an unhappy child needs things to do to feel engaged and useful. That said, it is a very difficult problem and a lot of people need to be involved to save the child.

Q: Did you experience bullying in your early life?

A: Sure, I was bullied in elementary and middle school. It wasn't physical bullying, but more teasing and insults. I was an un-athletic, intellectual child, and the kids who picked on me liked to remind me of it. Fortunately, I was never pushed around or beaten up or robbed, or things would have been worse. It was psychological abuse.

Q: If so, how did it make you feel (mentally, physically, emotionally, and spiritually)?

A: I felt weak, ashamed, and isolated. I wanted to keep to myself and just be left alone. I sought escape in reading and creative projects. I liked to be alone in my room with my books, my typewriter, and my toys.

Q: Did you have any outlets for your emotions when you were young?

A: Reading, listening to music, and playing with toys were my outlets. I worked out my emotions in these places and could usually get the bullying out of my mind.

Writing, and thinking about my characters and their stories, became outlets once I began to write novels when I was about 14.

"Music is the shorthand of emotion." ~ Leo Tolstoy (Russian novelist and philosopher)

I'll take some extra time to talk about music. I remember listening to my favorite music on LPs before leaving for school each day to give me strength to deal with the stress of the school day. I think kids still do this today—they rely upon music. They walk around school and the streets with earbuds or headphones in place, and when they are in class, they want to keep those earbuds as close as possible, in or hanging on top of their ears, or those headphones around their necks, to remind them that the music will soon be near. Today's kids just want music all the time. Being a mean teacher, I make them put away their musical devices. Did I mention that I'm mean? Grrr.

Q: Were you able to ask for help in recovering from the bullying?

A: In elementary school, I could get help from teachers; by middle school it was for me to manage on my own. I focused on self-soothing. By this I mean that I found ways to calm myself and steady my nerves, or at least to find the strength to tolerate. This involved music, as I have said elsewhere, as well as an active inner life converting my emotions into creative energy. I had to steel myself as best I could for each potentially difficult day. Anxiety about being bullied is perhaps as bad as the actual experience, because the anxiety goes on a lot longer and doesn't really go away so long as the potential exists for the bully to strike again. But, overall, I feel like I did all right. I knew my parents had supportive intentions, but I wasn't receptive to their advice and had to figure it out on my own.

Q: What steps did you take to recover? How did you try to increase your confidence? Your feeling of safety in the world? Your ability to trust other people?

A: I ended my experience of being bullied by getting rid of some of my eccentricities—carrying a lunchbox, refusing to wear blue jeans—by standing up for myself in a few small confrontations, and then by getting a gym membership and beginning to develop my physical fitness. In tenth grade I joined the wrestling team, and from that point, once I was known as a wrestler and had the team as visible backup, there were no more problems. Being on the team for a highly physical sport worked to help me broaden my profile from a "nerd" to a well-rounded person. I tested myself physically, learned to be part of a team and to get acceptance from tough young men, and just became the sort of person who would not be bullied.

> **"This situation sucks, but it isn't forever. It doesn't define who you are now or who you will be."**
> ~ Matt Posner

Q: In your mind, what would be the most important thing to say to a young person who is being bullied?

A: I don't know what would be most important to say, but here is what I am able to say.

This situation sucks, but it isn't forever. It doesn't define who you are now or who you will be. Life is complicated and bad things are part of it. You have to work to find a solution, but even if that solution isn't obvious or easy, there is another solution that is always there, and that is time. This kind of stuff doesn't last forever. It's like a storm. It passes. Maybe it doesn't pass soon enough for someone suffering like you are, but it does pass, and then your ability to do good things for others and for yourself will define the next part of your life.

Q: Do you have any thoughts on what school systems could do to stop bullying and violence in our schools?

A: My high school has a Peer Mediation program that works well to resolve both bullying and other forms of dispute between students. I would recommend Peer Mediation for any school with students old enough to learn how to do it. Peer Mediation can't settle all bullying situations, but it does work sometimes

Peer Mediation is a program we use at selected schools in New York City. In the program, the young adults who are quarreling are brought to a special room with a student who has been trained as a mediator. The mediator asks the youths to express their thoughts and feelings in this safe environment, and confirms that each of them understands the other's feelings. Most fights between those on the same social level can be resolved this way when the issues are aired and misunderstandings are cleared.

It sometimes helps with bullying, too, in that it may help the bully and the victim to understand each other, so that the oppositional relationship no longer feels comfortable or natural. It doesn't always work to stop bullying, but it's the best thing a school is likely to be able to offer, other than hitting the bully with such severe penalties that she or he doesn't consider that particular victim worth it anymore. That, of course, has lots of downsides, so it's good to peer-mediate first.

Here's a web link with some good information on the process: http://peermediation.pottsgrove.wikispaces.net/

For other bullying situations, I would recommend greater quantity and quality of counseling services—more social workers and more time for them to help!

~

Many thanks to Matt for sharing his wisdom and experience!

~

Some teachers are not very willing to talk about issues related to bullying, but many teachers like Matt are open to listening to your thoughts and feelings, and want to help. Keep asking until you find someone to listen to you.

Suggestions for Teachers

If you're a student, you might think about printing these pages and offering them to your teachers. Integrating an understanding of emotions into classwork will help everyone understand themselves and others better.

I propose that teachers begin to open a conversation about emotions with their students. If teens know that it's normal and acceptable to have emotions and express them in a healthy way, they're less likely to bully others or cause harm to themselves.

Here are some suggestions for integrating the subject into classwork:

- Ask students which feelings surface for them in response to a particular passage in a reading assignment, whether it's for history, English, a language class, or another subject.
- Create a writing exercise for an English class encouraging students to write about something that stimulates an emotional response—positive or negative. Arousing love and compassion is just as important as releasing difficult feelings.
- Art, music, and theater teachers have an unparalleled opportunity to help students understand that emotion is normal—in fact, it's part of what draws us to the arts. Invite the students' responses to artworks, encourage them to talk about their feeling response to music, and discuss what kinds of feelings might be motivating a particular character in a play.
- Social studies teachers can open a discussion about what people might have felt in response to historical events such as 9/11, and science teachers could construct a short module on psychology—a social science—in relation to emotion.

- Even physical education teachers can invite a short discussion about the contrast in feelings between winning and losing a game. Helping team members to let go of their frustration or gloom when they've lost a game can encourage them to think more positively about the possibility of winning the next game.

If discussions about bullying are already a part of your school culture, make sure that information about coping with feelings is also provided, along with suggestions for safe places to talk about them (for instance, with a school counselor or nurse—teachers too, if possible—or implement a peer mediation program).

Don't be afraid to let students know that your own emotions are stirred by circumstances and events. Students learn what teachers model—and discovering that emotions are normal and acceptable allows them to feel hope for their own situations.

Here are some suggestions for coping with bullying in your class or school:

- Place multiple well-marked drop boxes throughout the school where students can report incidents of harassment and bullying that they have experienced or witnessed. Assign someone to monitor the boxes every three hours, and make sure bullies know that their victims can report harassment in this way.
- Bullying can be a desperate bid for attention. Consider meeting early in the school year with students who have exhibited bullying behavior at the school in the past, and offer them appropriate channels of preventative support and intervention to them for the upcoming school year. Also, make sure that kids who have been bullied have access to support.
- Make sure that kids who have been bullied have access to support, and that they know there are people who will listen to them if they bring up bullying incidents.

Helpful Resources and Links

You can find a list of Hotlines to call on pages 39-40.

Web links:

Bullying:
http://www.bullying.co.uk/
http://www.bulliedgirl.com/
http://www.takeastandtogether.gov.au/index.html
http://www.antibullying.net/youngpeople.htm
http://www.beatbullying.org/

Building Self-Esteem:
http://www.spiritwire.com/selfesteemtips.html
http://www.lyndonantcliff.com/marketing/positive-
    thinking/ten-quick-tips-to-improve-your-self-esteem/
http://kidshealth.org/teen/your_mind/emotions/self_esteem.h
    tml#—This is a three-part article which offers an explanation
    of self-esteem and a list of steps you can take to build your
    self-esteem (page 3)
http://jeremyhubert.com/articles/10-tips-to-improve-your-self-
    esteem.html
http://www.wikihow.com/Develop-Self-Esteem

Websites for Parents:
http://www.awareparenting.com/

Books:
*Finding Your Own North Star: Claiming the Life You Were
    Meant to Live* by Martha Beck
*The Highly Sensitive Person: How to Thrive When the World
    Overwhelms You* by Elaine Aron
Are You Really Too Sensitive? by Marcy Calhoun
Subtle Energy by William Collinge, Ph.D.
*Warming the Stone Child: Abandonment and the Unmothered
    Child*—a wonderful and supportive audio recording by
    Clarissa Pinkola Estés, Ph.D.

Mother Night—another great supportive audio recording by Clarissa Pinkola Estés, Ph.D. which will help you build your self-esteem no matter who you are or what you believe
Creative Visualization by Shakti Gawain
Ask and It is Given by Abraham Hicks
Stick Up for Yourself: Every Kid's Guide to Personal Power & Positive Self-Esteem by Gershen Kaufman, Lev Raphael and Pamela Espeland
The Box of Daughter by Katherine Mayfield
Dysfunctional Families: The Truth Behind the Happy Family Façade by Katherine Mayfield
The Field by Lynne McTaggart
The Drama of the Gifted Child by Alice Miller
For Your Own Good by Alice Miller
Teen Guide to Sex and Relationships by Matt Posner and Jess C. Scott
Take Charge of Your Life: How Not to Be a Victim by Louis Proto
Bullies Are a Pain in the Brain by Trevor Romain
The Empowered Mind by Gini Graham Scott
Authentic Happiness by Martin Seligman
Learned Optimism by Martin Seligman (about overcoming learned helplessness)
Cyberslammed: Understand, Prevent, Combat, Transform the Most Common Cyberbullying Tactics by Kay Stephens and Vinitha Nair
Life Your Way by Amy Wood, Psy.D.

Appendix

A Short Meditation to Help You
Get in Touch with Yourself and Draw in Energy

This meditation is best practiced when you can find a quiet, safe place where you won't be disturbed.

1. Find a comfortable position. Sit in a way that fully supports your body.
2. Take a couple of deep, slow breaths, and let them out slowly. Let any tension go out of your body as you exhale.
3. Close your eyes and focus your attention on the inside of your body—think about your heart beating in your chest, your brain and nervous system continually sending signals back and forth. Take a couple of minutes to look and listen around the inside of your body.
4. Now place your focus outside of your body, and think about where your body is in relation to the whole world, the whole universe. Think about the stars way out in space—there is unlimited energy in between you and the world, you and the stars, just there for the taking.
5. See if you can feel this energy all around you. Think about how the wind moves tree branches, even though we can't see it, and how waves in the ocean keep moving all the time as the tides ebb and flow. These movements are expressions of the energy that flows through the universe all the time, everywhere. You are a part of this energy, too. See if you can feel the movement of this energy in your body.
6. As you take another deep breath, imagine that you're drawing the energy of the universe into your body and mind, as if your thoughts are sweeping the energy toward you, and allow it to "collect" in your body. When you breathe out, imagine that you're releasing whatever emotion is getting in your way, whether it's sadness, fear, anger, or whatever. Just let it flow out on your breath.
7. Think about what you want to draw in—it could be feelings of peace, it could be good friends, it could be more

respectful attention from others—and what you want to let go of as you continue to breathe in and out.

8. When you feel ready, open your eyes and take a couple of moments to reorient yourself to the space you're in. Take a moment to stretch your body.

This meditation can also be used with an affirmation, such as "I am breathing in peace, I am breathing out despair," or "I am breathing in protection, I am breathing out fear." You can breathe in energy wherever you are, whatever you're doing—but it's a good idea to practice first by sitting quietly in a safe place so you can get a feel for what it's like to be "full" of energy. This meditation is based on the principles of Qi Gong.

This universal energy is available whenever you want to tune in to it. Different cultures call it by different names: for instance, the Chinese call this energy "qi," and Native Americans refer to it as "Great Spirit."

> **"Albert Einstein showed through physics what the sages have taught for thousands of years: everything in our material world—animate and inanimate—is made of energy, and everything *radiates* energy."**
> ~ William Collinge, Ph.D., *Subtle Energy*

You can use this meditation wherever you are, whenever you feel yourself getting upset during the day. You can go within when you feel like you need encouragement, and tell yourself, "You're doing fine. You did a great job with that. Things will get better."

We can't always count on encouragement and support from others, but we can always give it to ourselves. It feels funny at first, and it will never replace your connections with other people, but learning to draw in energy and encourage yourself can help you feel stronger and more in charge of your life physically, mentally, emotionally, and spiritually.

Acknowledgments

So many people supported the idea of *Bullied* during the writing process—I deeply appreciate the encouragement for my work that has come from people in every corner of my life. I'd like to offer my very special thanks to the four people who graciously gave their time and offered their experience for the interviews: Michelle Baker, Amy Wood, Kathi Dezenzo, and Matt Posner. Thanks also to Darcy Scott and Matt Posner for their input on the manuscript and other aspects of the publishing process, and to Jennifer Caven of Mainly Words for editing and making suggestions which helped *Bullied* to become a better book. I'd also like to thank Martha Beck and William Collinge for granting permission to include their quotes in the book, and David and the great crew at Maine Authors Publishing for all the help putting the book together. You're all awesome!

Several organizations and individual people contributed to the development of *Bullied* through the Indiegogo campaign I implemented in the fall of 2012, and I gratefully acknowledge their contributions and support: Dare Family Services, Mainly Words Editing, Ark of Hope for Children, Darcy Scott, Mimi Watroba, Jeffrey Haste of Deerbrook Editions Press, Marilyn Mullins, and Emily Rosemary Thompson.

I'd also like to thank all the teachers, parents, school administrators, government officials, and other individuals and organizations who are taking steps to eradicate bullying. Thanks also to Elinor, who reminded me that teachers and coaches can also be bullies, and to the websites QuoteGarden.com, ThinkExist.com, BrainyQuote.com, and SearchQuotes.com for providing a compendium of great quotes. And I'm eternally grateful to the muse who consistently and excitedly fuels my work with new ideas and better ways of expressing them. I only hope I can keep up.

If you found *Bullied* helpful, please consider sharing the word via Facebook and Twitter, blogging about the book, or writing a book review on Amazon, Goodreads, or BarnesandNoble.com.

We need to help as many teens as we possibly can.

Many thanks!

About the Author

A former actress who appeared Off-Broadway and on the daytime drama Guiding Light, Katherine Mayfield is the author of the award-winning memoir *The Box of Daughter: Healing the Authentic Self*, two books on the acting business: *Smart Actors, Foolish Choices* and *Acting A to Z*, both published by Back Stage Books, and the Kindle book *Dysfunctional Families: The Truth Behind the Happy Family Facade*.

Ms. Mayfield's memoir *The Box of Daughter* won the Bronze Medal in the 2012 Reader's Favorite Book Awards, an Honorable Mention in the 2012 New England Book Festival, and was nominated as a Finalist in the Maine Literary Awards. *The Box of Daughter* was inspired by the title poem in her book of poems, *The Box of Daughter and Other Poems*.

Ms. Mayfield has presented workshops in Maine and Massachusetts, is a member of Maine Writers and Publishers Alliance, and speaks regularly at the Portsmouth Athenæum's Wednesday Writers' Series in Portsmouth, NH.

Websites:
www.TheBoxofDaughter.com
www.Katherine-Mayfield.com

Social Media:
Twitter: K_Mayfield
Facebook: KatherineMayfieldauthor

About Michelle Baker, Author of the Foreword

In addition to being a writer, Ms. Baker is a visual and performing artist. She is Educational Director of Blaze My Trail youth program, and currently lives in Asheville, NC with her awesome son and their frisky Siamese cat.